COUNTRY ELEGANCE

COTTON AND WOOL PROJECTS FROM THE QUILTED CROW GIRLS

Leonie Bateman and Deirdre Bond-Abel

Martingale®

Create with Confidence

Dedications

Again, to my beautiful family—Dan, Ellen, and Jess—whose love and support in everything I do allows me to continue to follow my dream. Without your continued love and support, I wouldn't be the person I am today. I am so proud of you all—you mean the world to me and I love you to the moon and back, and then some.

~ Leonie

To my husband, Phil, and my children, Casey and Mitchell, thank you for your continued love and support.

~ Deirdre

Country Elegance: Cotton and Wool Projects
from the Quilted Crow Girls
© 2014 by Leonie Bateman and Deirdre Bond-Abel

Martingale®
19021 120th Ave. NE, Ste. 102
Bothell, WA 98011-9511 USA
ShopMartingale.com

Printed in China
19 18 17 16 15 14   8 7 6 5 4 3 2 1

Library of Congress Cataloging-in-Publication Data is available upon request.

ISBN: 978-1-60468-405-6

MISSION STATEMENT

Dedicated to providing quality products and service to inspire creativity.

CREDITS

PRESIDENT AND CEO: Tom Wierzbicki
EDITOR IN CHIEF: Mary V. Green
DESIGN DIRECTOR: Paula Schlosser
MANAGING EDITOR: Karen Costello Soltys
ACQUISITIONS EDITOR: Karen M. Burns
TECHNICAL EDITOR: Ellen Pahl
COPY EDITOR: Tiffany Mottet
PRODUCTION MANAGER: Regina Girard
COVER DESIGNER: Paula Schlosser
INTERIOR DESIGNER: Adrienne Smitke
PHOTOGRAPHER: Brent Kane
ILLUSTRATOR: Christine Erikson

Acknowledgments

We'd both like to thank the team at Martingale for their continued support and for giving us the opportunity to work with them again. Each person goes above and beyond to make everything just right. We can't thank you all enough for everything you do. We're just so chuffed!

CONTENTS

INTRODUCTION

Come on another journey with us as we share with you our love of quiltmaking and working with felted wool. Inspiration is all around us in our daily lives, from old tiles and wallpapers to antique quilts and beautiful iron fretwork on historical buildings, and we love to incorporate elements of these things into our work.

We've both been designing, traveling, and teaching for many years now, sharing our techniques and love of combining two of our favorite mediums—felted wool and reproduction fabrics. Our styles are quite similar, but we each design our own work separately—there have been occasions where we have come up with a design and it's pretty close to what the other was thinking, which goes to show how alike our tastes are.

Our shop, The Quilted Crow, is located in historic Hobart, the capital city of Tasmania, Australia. Housed in a beautiful old sandstone church built in 1865, it is filled with all the things that make our hearts sing—beautiful displays, old bits of furniture, and many other needful treasures.

We hope you continue to enjoy the journey with us as we share our love of working with wool and reproduction fabrics.

~ Leonie and Deirdre

Appliqué

Many of our projects feature appliqué—some with cotton, some with wool, and some with both!

APPLIQUÉING WITH WOOL

Once you start working with this wonderful medium, you won't look back! Wool is one of our favorite mediums to work with and, when combined with reproduction fabrics, designs can look a real treat.

Once wool has been felted, the edges won't fray, so you don't need to turn them under. The following section covers the techniques we use for preparing appliqués and positioning them on the background fabric, the tools and supplies we like, and some of our favorite stitches.

What Is Felted Wool?

First, let's explain the differences between felted wool and wool felt. Felted wool is a *woven* wool fabric that's washed and agitated in hot water and dried with heat. This process condenses and compacts (felts) the fibers and results in a lovely soft and fluffy fabric that won't fray. Projects made with felted wool can be laundered without the worry of the pieces shrinking or fraying.

Wool felt, on the other hand, is made up of individual wool fibers that have been wetted, heated, and tightly compressed together, as opposed to woven together. Wool felt cannot be laundered as successfully as felted wool. Always read the label before purchasing wool felt, as not all wool felt is 100% wool. Some are made up of a blend of wool and other fibers. While these are okay to use for our projects, the drape and feel of the fabric won't be the same as when using felted wool.

Choosing Wool for Appliqué

We use only felted wool made from 100% wool fibers. When choosing wool for appliqué, look for wool that isn't too thick, and choose a variety of colors and textures that will add visual interest to your work.

Hand-dyed wools are great to have in your wool stash. Because they're hand dyed, there can be many subtle variations in color within a piece, which is a good thing—use the light and dark sections from a hand-dyed piece to create a flower or a leaf and see how different it can look than if you use a solid color. Different patterns, such as plaid or herringbone, are great for adding visual texture to backgrounds, large leaves, or pots. And make sure you include some "uglies" (wool pieces in patterns and colors you might not like on their own) in your stitched piece. Just as with cotton fabrics, the unexpected element can sometimes add just the right touch to make a piece pop.

Preparing Wool for Appliqué

When we receive wool fabric in our shop, the first thing we do is take it home and put it through the felting process. Doing this ensures that the wool is ready to use in a project. We suggest that when you purchase wool, find out if it has already been felted. If it hasn't, then we recommend you launder it as soon as you get home, bearing in mind that it's going to shrink.

As an example, let's assume that you have a 24" x 54" piece of unfelted woven wool. When you purchase wool yardage from the bolt, it is generally 54" wide. After you put it through a hot wash and dryer, it will shrink to approximately 20" x 48". All of the wool yardage requirements in our book are based on wool that has been felted and is 48" wide.

Threads and Tools for Wool Appliqué

In addition to the tools and supplies you need for regular quilting, you'll need some specific threads and tools for wool appliqué. Below are some of our favorites:

- ❧ Aurifil 28-weight Cotton Mako thread
- ❧ Size 11 milliner's needles and/or size 8 appliqué needles for hand sewing
- ❧ 4" fine-point embroidery scissors. This size is ideal for cutting tiny shapes and for cutting out shapes for reverse appliqué.
- ❧ Water-soluble glue stick
- ❧ General office stapler. We use this to temporarily attach appliqués to the background fabric. A 12" office stapler is also good to have on hand because the extra length makes it much easier to reach into places that a standard-size stapler can't.
- ❧ Marking tools: white pencil or marker, water-soluble marker, lead pencil
- ❧ Freezer paper
- ❧ Light box
- ❧ Rotary-cutting equipment

Making a Master Pattern

Several of the appliqué designs in this book can be positioned by simply eyeballing the flowers, leaves, or stems. Other designs require symmetry to achieve a balanced look. For example, you may want to have the same sweep of the vine on all four of a quilt's appliquéd borders. The best way to make sure each piece is the same is to make a master pattern. Simply trace the pattern for the desired project onto a piece of paper (copy paper is fine) using a lead pencil. You'll then be able to center your background fabric over the master pattern and use it as a guide for placing the appliqués.

Because several of the patterns are too large to fit on one sheet of paper, you'll need to trace each individual section onto its own piece of paper, and then join the sections where indicated to make a complete pattern. Be sure to transfer the reference lines to the master pattern.

Making the Appliqués

We both use freezer paper to make templates for cutting the appliqué shapes. The beauty of freezer paper is that you can reuse the templates a number of times before they no longer adhere to the wool and need to be replaced. Start by tracing one of each shape and make more as needed.

> ### GET MORE MILEAGE FROM FREEZER PAPER
> Reuse freezer paper from larger pieces to trace a smaller pattern template inside the edges. Keep reusing the paper until it becomes too fuzzy. Then it's time to toss it.

1. Trace each shape onto the dull side of a piece of freezer paper, leaving approximately ¼" to ½" between the shapes. Using paper scissors, roughly cut out each shape. With the shiny side down, iron each shape onto the right side of the selected piece of wool using a dry iron. Try not to press too hard on the wool so that you don't flatten the fabric too much.

2. Carefully cut out each piece along the drawn line and remove the freezer paper. Your shapes are now ready for placement onto your background piece.

> ### FREEZER PAPER TO THE RESCUE
> In some cases, it's a good idea to leave your freezer paper on the fabric so that it acts as a stabilizer when applying the glue. This is especially helpful when your shapes have cutout areas, as it prevents the wool from curling up or stretching.

Cutting Stems and Vines

The beauty of working with wool is that it curves nicely, without the need to cut it on the bias. The curve of the stems and vines in the appliqué patterns are for placement only. You do not need to trace the stems and cut freezer-paper patterns. All stems and vines are rotary cut on the straight of grain and measurements are included where necessary in the cutting instructions for each design.

Preparing the Background for Appliqué

We prefer to align appliqué pieces precisely, so we mark reference lines on the background fabric to help us be consistent. To do this, we simply fold the background fabric in half vertically and horizontally or diagonally in both directions, depending on the design, and finger-press the folds. Often we mark over the fold lines with a water-soluble marker or white pencil or marker (for dark fabrics) so the lines are easier to see.

Some people prefer to place their appliqué pieces by eye and do not use any reference lines. This method works well too. After all, if we look at a flowering plant in the garden, it grows in all different directions. The same can be said for appliqué—it doesn't have to be exact.

Appliquéing Wool to the Background

After all the shapes are cut out and the background is prepared, it's time to position and appliqué the motifs. The following is our favorite method for temporarily holding the appliqués in place until they've been stitched. Some people are shocked when we tell them we use a water-soluble glue stick and an office stapler, but it works! Neither of us likes to use any sort of fusible web to attach our pieces, so the glue-and-stapler method is a great alternative for us. The staples are easy to remove with your fingers and because wool is self-healing, there aren't any marks that remain on the appliqués.

1. Place the master pattern on a light box. Position the background fabric right side up over the pattern, aligning all reference points.

> **PREASSEMBLING UNITS**
>
> For appliqués that are made up of more than one piece, such as the center flower in "Dickinson" (page 31), stitch the pieces together, and then stitch the assembled unit to the background piece. It's easier to stitch one assembled unit to the background than to stitch each piece individually.

2. Apply a dab of glue to the wrong side of each appliqué shape or preassembled unit. Follow the master pattern to gently press the shapes into place on the background, working from the bottom layer up. You can also use a glue stick along the length of stems and vines—gently run the glue along the strip, and then press a nice smooth curve into the wool following the outline on your pattern.

3. Once all of the pieces are in place, staple them for a firm hold. We've found that if we just rely on the glue, it isn't enough to keep the pieces in place when we're handling the project during the appliqué process. Give stapling a try—you'll be surprised at the result!

4. Use a blanket stitch to appliqué the pieces in place using matching thread and your needle of choice. Refer to "Stitching Details" on page 8 for additional guidance. When appliqués are secured, remove the staples.

STITCHING DETAILS

After experimenting with many different brands of thread, we chose Aurifil 28-weight Cotton Mako thread as our preferred thread for our appliqué. The thickness of the 28-weight is ideal for the small stitches that we both like to take on our work; it is a one-stranded thread, so there's no need to separate strands. It just glides through the wool with no splitting or twisting. The color range is vast and, to top it off, it's also a multi-purpose thread—it can also be used in your sewing machine! When Leonie wants more definition, such as in "A Little Bird Told Me" (page 21), she uses two strands of thread or floss. She uses a size 11 milliner's needle for all of her appliqué and Deirdre uses a size 8 appliqué needle. We suggest you experiment with different threads and needles and use what works best for you.

We stitch all of our appliqué using a blanket stitch. When blanket-stitching pieces to the background, don't pull the thread up too tight, or the edges of the wool will curl up. Just let your thread rest on top of the appliqué. When we're blanket-stitching through multiple layers, we find that a stab stitch keeps our work nice and flat.

Occasionally some of our projects have a few embroidery elements that require the use of other stitches. The stitches we commonly use are shown below.

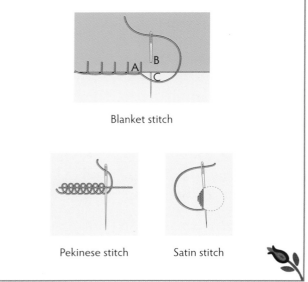

Blanket stitch

Pekinese stitch   Satin stitch

APPLIQUÉING A DOGTOOTH BORDER

Don't be intimidated by the dogtooth border used in "Mangal's Visit" (page 45). The border is relatively easy to make; it just takes a little time and patience. Like anything, after you've done it once, it will become much easier! The main thing is to be very careful when cutting out the pieces.

Cutting the Border Strips

1. Trace the dogtooth border pattern onto the dull side of a piece of freezer paper, repeating the design to extend the pattern to the length given. The borders will be cut longer than needed. Ensure that the piece of wool you're using for the dogtooth border has straight edges.

2. With the shiny side down, align the straight edge of the freezer-paper pattern with the edge of the wool and iron the pattern in place.

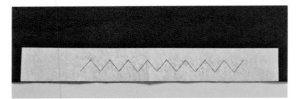

Align the edge of the freezer paper with the straight edge of the wool.

3. Very carefully cut out the border using a pair of scissors with sharp points. Take care when cutting dogtooth borders so that you can use the adjacent piece (shown at the top in the photo below) for the opposite side border. Remove the freezer paper from the lower border piece only.

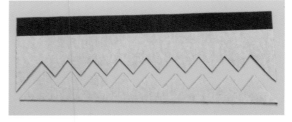

The border is on the bottom; the piece along the top will be used for the opposite dogtooth border.

4. To cut the remaining side border, lay the remaining piece from step 3 on your rotary cutting mat. Align the ½" line of your rotary ruler with the inner points of the piece; cut along the straight edge of the ruler.

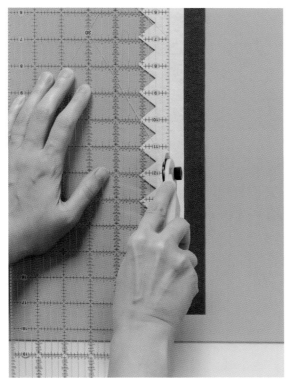

Cut ½" from the inner points of the leftover dogtooth-border piece to make the opposite side border.

5. Repeat steps 1–4 to make the top and bottom borders.

Positioning the Border Strips

1. Fold the background fabric in half vertically and horizontally and finger-press the folds.

2. Mark a reference line around the edge of the background fabric, as described in the project instructions. These lines will form a frame and act as a guide to place the border strips.

3. Place a border strip on the appropriate edge of the background. Center the top point of a dogtooth border on the center fold line of the background fabric. Place the inner points of the border strip right on top of the drawn reference line. You'll have excess at one or both ends, which will be trimmed away later.

Align the center top point of the border with the center fold line of the background fabric. Position the inner points on the drawn line.

4. Repeat steps 1–3 for the remaining sides. It doesn't matter in which order you place them. Make sure there are no openings in the "frame." The ends that overlap at the corners will be trimmed after the border is appliquéd in place. Once you're happy with the placement, hold the strips in place with a dab of fabric glue and some staples.

5. Appliqué the decorative edge of each border strip. Trim the excess so the edges just overlap each other. Remove the staples.

REVERSE APPLIQUÉ

Many of our designs feature reverse appliqué, which simply means that we cut out a section of the main appliqué and slip another fabric between the background fabric and the appliqué so that a second color shows through. By incorporating these cutout areas, we're able to easily add extra color and dimension to a design. In some designs you'll find we placed wool behind wool, which gives a three-dimensional look; for other designs we used cotton behind the wool. Either way, reverse appliqué provides a look that's visually pleasing.

1. Refer to "Making the Appliqués" (page 6) to make the main shape from wool. Cut away the areas indicated using your embroidery scissors.

2. Cut a piece of wool or cotton that's larger than the main shape and place it under the main shape so that the right side is visible through the

cutout areas. Use a couple of dabs of glue and some staples to hold it in place.

Place the wool appliqué shape with the cutouts onto a larger piece of wool or cotton fabric.

3. Blanket-stitch around the inside edges of the cutout areas to attach the two pieces.

Blanket-stitch the inside edges.

4. Trim the larger background piece so there isn't any fabric showing around the main shape.

Trim the background piece.

NEEDLE-TURN APPLIQUÉ

Combining needle-turn appliqué of cotton fabrics with wool appliqué creates some great results. Leonie has combined both in her project "A Simple Life" on page 27.

1. Trace the large and small circles from the pattern on page 30 onto freezer paper and cut out on the drawn line.

2. Iron the freezer-paper templates onto the right side of the fabric. Using a white pencil or other marking tool of your choice, mark around the freezer-paper template and peel the freezer paper away. Cut around the circles leaving approximately ⅛" seam allowance.

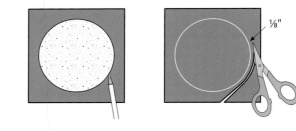

3. Position the piece in place on the design with a couple of dabs of appliqué glue.

4. Using your needle, turn under a small section along the drawn line and hold in place with your non-sewing hand. Using a matching thread bring your needle up from the bottom of your work in between the folded edge. Insert the needle into the background close to where the thread came out of the fold and take a small stitch, approximately ¹⁄₁₆", coming up again into the folded edge.

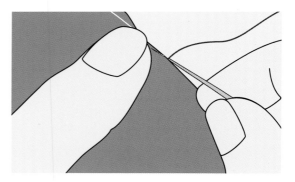

5. Continue working in this way, sweeping under the edge of the fabric with your needle as you go, being careful not to fray the edges with your needle.

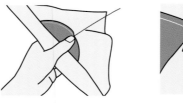

Machine Piecing and Finishing

We love appliqué, but we do include pieced blocks in many projects, and at some point, we have to sew blocks together, add borders, and finish our quilts! Here are the basic techniques that will enable you to complete all of the projects in this book.

QUICK CORNER TRIANGLES

Several of the designs in this book are pieced using the quick-corner-triangles method. This involves using a larger square or rectangle and a smaller square to produce a triangle or angled corner.

1. On the wrong side of the smaller square, draw a diagonal line from corner to corner.

2. Place the marked piece on one corner of the larger square or rectangle, right sides together. Sew on the drawn line.

3. Trim away the outside layers ¼" from the stitching line.

4. Press the resulting triangle away from the larger piece.

Several of the designs will also have another square sewn to the opposite side of the larger piece, but the angle of the resulting triangle will run in the opposite direction.

HALF-SQUARE-TRIANGLE UNITS

This method of making half-square-triangle units minimizes stretching the bias edge of the squares and produces two identical half-square-triangle units for each pair of squares used.

1. Cut two contrasting squares to the size needed. Draw a diagonal line from corner to corner on the wrong side of the lighter-colored square.

2. Place the squares right sides together with the marked square on top and the edges aligned.

3. Sew ¼" from both sides of the drawn line.

4. Cut on the drawn line to create two half-square-triangle units. Press the seam allowances toward the darker fabric in each unit.

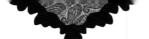

QUARTER-SQUARE-TRIANGLE UNITS

One of the designs in this book uses the quarter-square-triangle method. This involves placing two squares together and, once sewn, cutting twice to produce an Hourglass block.

1. On the wrong side of a square, draw a diagonal line from corner to corner in both directions.

2. Place the marked piece on an unmarked square, right sides together. Sew ¼" from both sides of *one* diagonal line.

3. Cut along the *unsewn* diagonal line first, leave the pieces in place, and then cut along the sewn diagonal line. Press the seam allowances toward the darker fabric.

4. Match the pieced triangles up so that the matching fabrics are diagonally opposite each other and sew into a square to make an Hourglass block. Press the seam allowances in one direction.

QUILTING

We've used a variety of quilting styles on the designs in this book. Some are quilted on our long-arm quilting machine; other projects are hand quilted or quilted using a combination of both hand and machine methods. Choose whichever method you prefer.

PIPING

Piping is fun and easy to make once you learn how. You can take a plain-looking pillow and turn it into something so much better just by adding some piping in a contrasting color. Once you start, you'll want to add piping to all of the pillows you make in the future!

For her pillow "A Little Bird Told Me" on page 21, Leonie used cotton cording, ¼" thick, which she purchased from a drapery store.

It's always wise when making piping, to cut your fabric strips on the bias so that you achieve nice, smooth curves on your corners. If you don't, you'll find that the corners will have "wrinkles" in them, and the result will not be as pleasing.

Making the Piping

1. Start by making a bias strip. Either cut 2"-wide bias strips individually and join them end to end, or use the continuous bias technique. (Go to ShopMartingale.com/HowtoQuilt for free downloadable information on making continuous bias. A 14" square will make approximately 60" of 2"-wide bias, enough for the pillow in this book.)

2. Starting ½" away from the folded end of your continuous bias strip, place the ¼"-thick cording inside the strip, against the center fold. Pin well.

3. Attach a zipper foot to your sewing machine and using a matching thread, commence stitching right up next to the cording, staying as close as you can to the cording. Continue stitching until you get to the end.

Attaching Piping

1. Starting in the center on the bottom of the pillow, pin the folded end of the piping to your pillow top piece, aligning the raw edges. Continue to pin all the way around, clipping into the seam allowances of the piping on the corners to allow the piping to ease around nicely. You will have excess at the end, which will be trimmed away later.

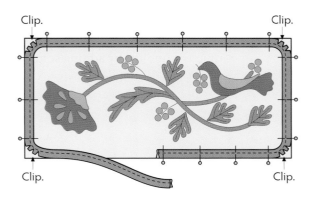

2. Begin stitching about ¾" from the beginning of the folded edge. Continue stitching, making sure that the stitching is right up against the cording.

3. When you are close to the end, cut the excess piping so that it meets the piping at the beginning and tuck it into the folded edge. Continue stitching to the end. Backstitch to reinforce the seam, and then remove the pillow from the machine.

BINDING

Unless otherwise indicated, binding strips are cut across the width of the fabric. We cut our strips 2¼" wide for a binding that finishes at approximately ⅜". You can cut your strips wider or narrower as desired. The strips are folded and sewn to the quilt to make a double-fold binding.

1. Follow the cutting instructions for each pattern to cut the required number of 2¼"-wide strips.

2. Join the strips end to end using a diagonal seam, and then trim away the excess fabric ¼" from the stitching lines. Press the seam allowances open.

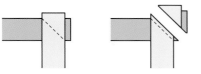

3. Press the beginning end of the strip at a 45° angle. Fold the fabric in half lengthwise, wrong sides together, and press the binding flat.

4. Beginning with the angled end, pin the binding to one side of the quilt top, aligning the raw edges. Using a ¼" seam allowance, begin sewing approximately 3" from the angled end and stop sewing ¼" from the first corner; backstitch.

5. Remove the quilt from the sewing machine. Fold the binding up at a 90° angle, and then bring it back down onto itself to square the corner. Begin stitching at the edge of the binding strip and stop sewing ¼" from the next corner. Repeat the folding and sewing process for each corner.

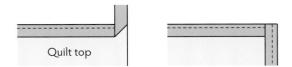

6. Keep sewing until you reach the beginning of the binding strip. Lap the end of the binding strip over the beginning about 2"; cut off the excess.

7. Tuck the tail of the binding inside the fold of the angled end, and then continue sewing until you reach the point where you began stitching; backstitch.

8. Fold the binding to the back of the quilt and pin it in place. Hand slip-stitch the fold of the binding to the back of the quilt.

MRS. B.

I truly adore four-block appliqué quilts, particularly antique ones. There's just something about them that makes my heart sing. Their design can be so simple, yet they always manage to make a strong statement. I don't think I'll ever tire of admiring or making four-block quilts. And who doesn't love that color combination of red, pink, and green with a touch of yellow? This one was made in honor of my wonderful mother-in-law, "Mrs. B.," whom I love so dearly.

~ Leonie

FINISHED QUILT: 58" x 58"

"Mrs. B.," designed, machine pieced, hand appliquéd, and hand quilted by Leonie Bateman

MATERIALS

Cotton Fabric

Yardage is based on 42"-wide fabric.

3⅓ yards of shirting print for appliquéd-block backgrounds and sashing

1⅞ yards of pink print for sashing, cornerstones, and binding

¼ yard of red print for leaf reverse-appliqué inserts

3⅔ yards of fabric for backing

Felted Wool Fabric

Yardage is based on 48"-wide fabric.

1 yard of green for leaves

½ yard of pink for corner flowers and center petals, scalloped center flower, and circle

½ yard of red for corner flowers, scalloped center flower, and center star

12" x 12" piece of antique gold for top of corner flowers

Additional Materials

Embroidery floss in colors to match wool fabrics

66" x 66" piece of batting

60" length of freezer paper

Water-soluble glue stick

Stapler

CUTTING

From the shirting print, cut:
4 squares, 22" x 22"
9 squares, 6½" x 6½"
120 rectangles, 2½" x 6½"

From the pink print, cut:
18 strips, 2½" x 42"; crosscut into 276 squares, 2½" x 2½"
7 strips, 2¼" x 42"

PREPARING FOR APPLIQUÉ

1. Fold each shirting-print 22" square in half vertically and horizontally and finger-press the folds. Fold each square in half diagonally in both directions and finger-press the folds. If desired, mark the fold lines with a water-soluble marker.

2. Refer to "Making a Master Pattern" (page 6) to make a master pattern using the patterns on pages 18 and 19.

3. Refer to "Making the Appliqués" (page 6) to trace all of the appliqué shapes onto freezer paper, roughly cut out the shapes, and then iron the freezer-paper shapes onto your chosen colors of wool. You'll need four sets of appliqué shapes for the blocks. Refer to the photo on page 14 and the materials list for fabric choices as needed. Cut out the wool shapes.

4. Refer to "Preassembling Units" (page 7) to assemble the scalloped center flower into a unit. Refer to "Reverse Appliqué" (page 9) to reverse appliqué the cutout sections of the leaves with the red cotton print.

ADDING THE APPLIQUÉS

1. Refer to "Appliquéing Wool to the Background" (page 7) to position the appliqués on each of the background squares, working from the bottom layer to the top. Glue and staple your prepared appliqué pieces in place.

2. Using your thread and needle of choice, appliqué the pieces in place with a blanket stitch (page 8). Remove the staples.

3. Trim the blocks to 20½" square, keeping the design centered.

MAKING THE SASHING

1. Draw a diagonal line from corner to corner on the wrong side of each pink 2½" square.

2. Referring to "Quick Corner Triangles" (page 11), place marked squares on opposite ends of a shirting-print 2½" x 6½" rectangle as shown. Sew on the marked lines. Trim the seam allowances to ¼". Press the triangles toward the corners. Make a total of 120 sashing units.

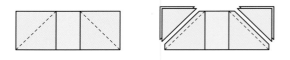

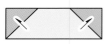

Make 120.

3. Place marked squares on each corner of a shirting-print 6½" square as shown. Sew, trim, and press as before. Make a total of nine cornerstone blocks.

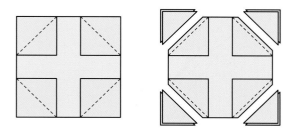

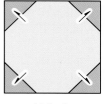

Make 9.

ASSEMBLING THE QUILT TOP

1. Sew 10 sashing units together as shown to make a sashing strip. Press the seam allowances in one direction. Make a total of 12 strips.

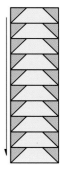

Make 12.

2. Alternately sew three sashing strips and two blocks together as shown. Press the seam allowances toward the blocks. Make a total of two block rows.

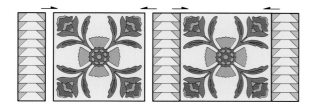

3. Alternately sew three cornerstone blocks and two sashing strips together as shown. Press the seam allowances toward the blocks to make a horizontal sashing strip. Make three strips.

Make 3.

4. Alternately sew the horizontal sashing strips and block rows together to complete the quilt top. Press the seam allowances toward the block rows.

Quilt assembly

FINISHING

1. Cut and piece the backing fabric so it's 4" larger than the quilt top on each side. Sandwich the batting between the backing and quilt top, and baste the layers together.

2. Quilt as desired. Leonie outline quilted the appliqués and quilted diagonal lines in the backgrounds of the appliquéd blocks. She quilted a Celtic design in the cornerstone blocks and outline quilted the sawtooth sashing.

3. Trim the backing and batting even with the quilt top. Refer to "Binding" (page 13) to bind the quilt edges with the pink 2¼"-wide strips.

> Align patterns as indicated to make a quarter pattern. Make four quarter patterns, and then join pieces to make complete pattern.

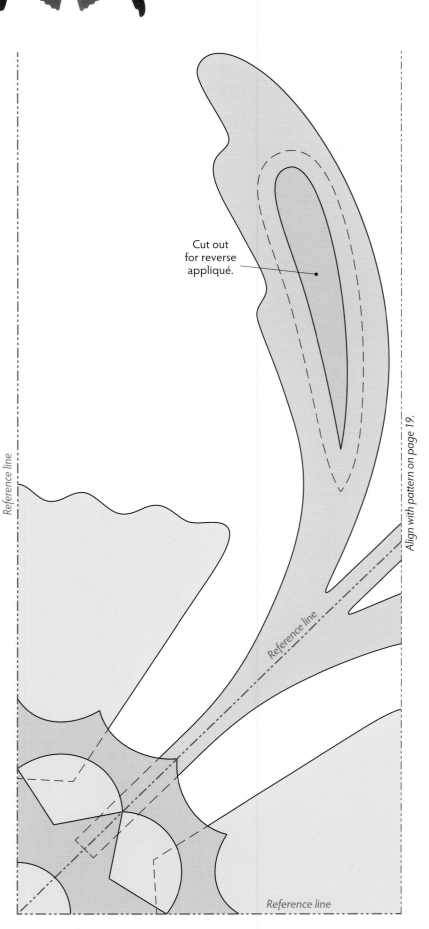

Cut out for reverse appliqué.

Reference line

Reference line

Align with pattern on page 19.

Reference line

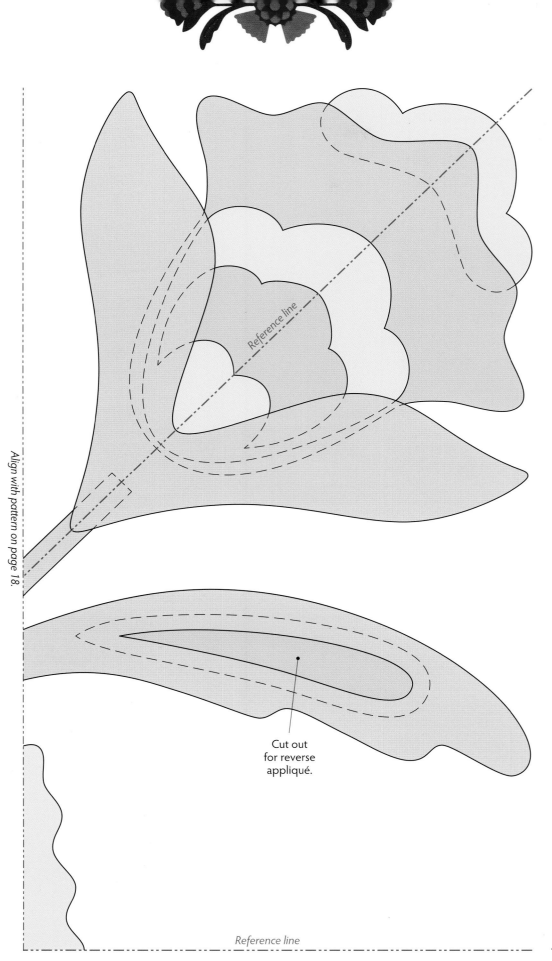

Align with pattern on page 18.

Reference line

Cut out
for reverse
appliqué.

A LITTLE BIRD TOLD ME

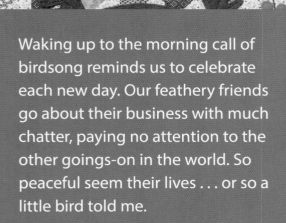

Waking up to the morning call of birdsong reminds us to celebrate each new day. Our feathery friends go about their business with much chatter, paying no attention to the other goings-on in the world. So peaceful seem their lives . . . or so a little bird told me.

~ Leonie

FINISHED PILLOW: 10" x 22"

"A Little Bird Told Me," designed, machine pieced, hand appliquéd, and machine quilted by Leonie Bateman

MATERIALS

Cotton Fabric

Yardage is based on 42"-wide fabric.

⅓ yard of shirting print for background and half-square triangles

Scraps, at least 3" x 15" *each* of 4 assorted pink and red prints for half-square triangles

20" x 20" square of red print for piping

14" x 26" piece of muslin for backing the pillow top

Felted Wool Fabric

Yardage is based on 48"-wide fabric.

1 fat quarter (18" x 24" piece) of red for pillow back, flower, and bird

3" x 24" piece of green for stems and leaves

5" x 5" piece of teal for reverse-appliqué inserts and berries

2" x 6" piece of antique gold for bird wing and flower base

Additional Materials

Embroidery floss in colors to match wool fabrics

14" x 26" piece of batting

Wool roving or polyester fiberfill for stuffing

2 yards of ¼"-diameter cotton cording for piping

12" length of freezer paper

Water-soluble glue stick

Water-soluble marker

Stapler

CUTTING

From the shirting print, cut:
1 rectangle, 8½" x 10½"
18 squares, 2⅞" x 2⅞"

From the assorted pink and red prints, cut a total of:
18 squares, 2⅞" x 2⅞"

From the green wool, cut:
1 strip, ⅜" x 24"; crosscut into:
    1 stem, ⅜" x 17"
    1 stem, ⅜" x 7"

From the red wool, cut:
1 rectangle, 10½" x 22½"

PREPARING FOR APPLIQUÉ

1. Mark a diagonal line from corner to corner on the wrong side of each of the shirting-print 2⅞" squares. (Refer to "Half-Square-Triangle Units" on page 11.) Place a marked square on top of a pink or red 2⅞" square, right sides together. Sew ¼" from both sides of the drawn line. Cut on the drawn line to create two half-square-triangle units. Press the seam allowances toward the darker triangle. Make a total of 36 half-square-triangle units (1 is extra).

Make 36.

2. Sew seven half-square-triangle units together with the darker fabric pointed in the same direction as shown to make one strip. Press the seam allowances toward the darker triangle. Make five strips.

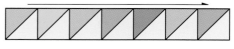

Make 5.

3. Join the five strips together as shown to form a pieced rectangle. Press the seam allowances in one direction.

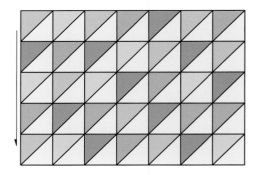

4. Join the shirting-print 8½" x 10½" rectangle to the pieced section and press the seam allowances toward the shirting-print rectangle.

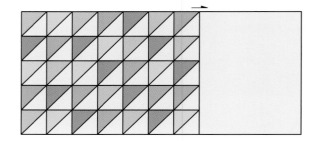

5. Fold the piece in half vertically and horizontally and finger-press the fold. Refer to "Making a Master Pattern" (page 6) to make a master pattern using the patterns on pages 24 and 25.

6. Refer to "Making the Appliqués" (page 6) to trace all of the appliqué shapes onto freezer paper, and iron the freezer-paper shapes onto your chosen colors of wool. Refer to the photo on page 20 and the materials list for fabric choices as needed. Cut out the wool shapes.

7. Refer to "Reverse Appliqué" (page 9) to reverse appliqué the cutout sections of the large flower.

8. Lay your master pattern on a light box or other light source and position the prepared background fabric on top of the master pattern, lining up the vertical center fold and the horizontal center fold of the background with the reference line on the master pattern.

ADDING THE APPLIQUÉS

1. Refer to "Appliquéing Wool to the Background" (page 7) to glue and staple your prepared appliqué pieces in place, working from the bottom layer to the top.

2. Once your appliqués are positioned, use a water-soluble marker and hand draw the stems for the berries.

3. Using your thread and needle of choice, appliqué the pieces in place with a blanket stitch (page 8). Remove the staples.

4. Mark the veins on the leaves with a white ceramic pencil or other marking tool of your choice. Use a Pekinese stitch (page 8) and two strands of your chosen thread to embroider the stems for the berries and the veins in the leaves.

FINISHING

1. Layer and baste the pillow top with the batting and muslin. Quilt around the appliqués using loops and swirls.

2. Trim the batting and muslin even with the pillow top.

3. Refer to "Piping" (page 12) to make 2 yards of piping using the red 20" square and the cotton cording. Attach the piping to the pillow front.

4. Lay the pillow front and red-wool 10½" x 22½" rectangle right sides together. Pin the front and back together.

5. Stitch the front to the back, leaving a 6" opening along the bottom. Turn the pillow cover right side out.

6. Firmly stuff the pillow with wool roving or polyester fiberfill, and then sew the opening closed by hand.

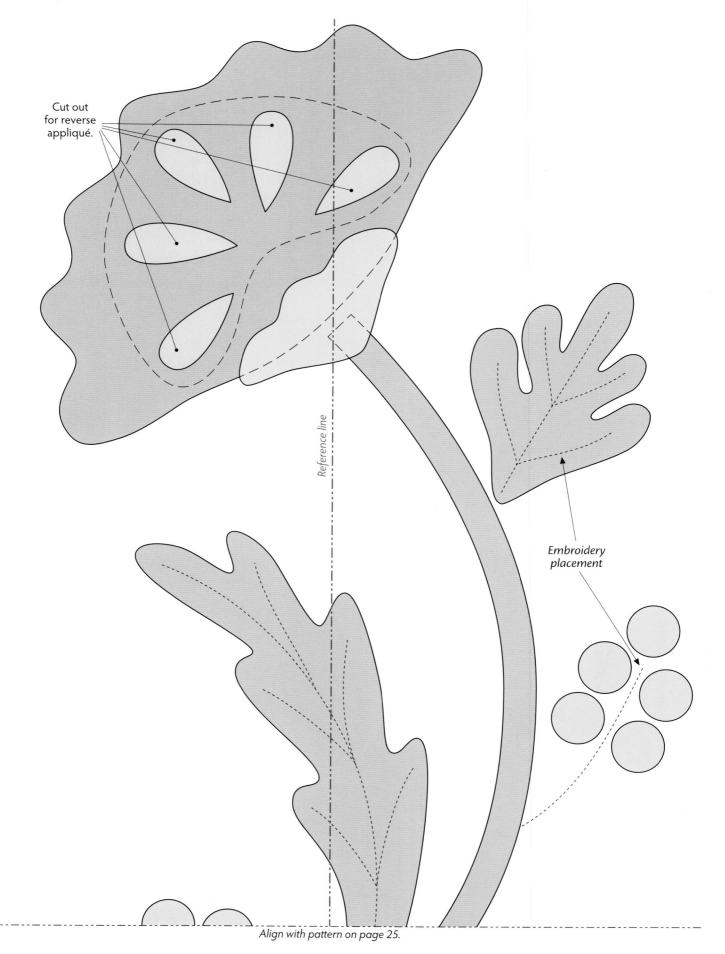

Cut out for reverse appliqué.

Reference line

Embroidery placement

Align with pattern on page 25.

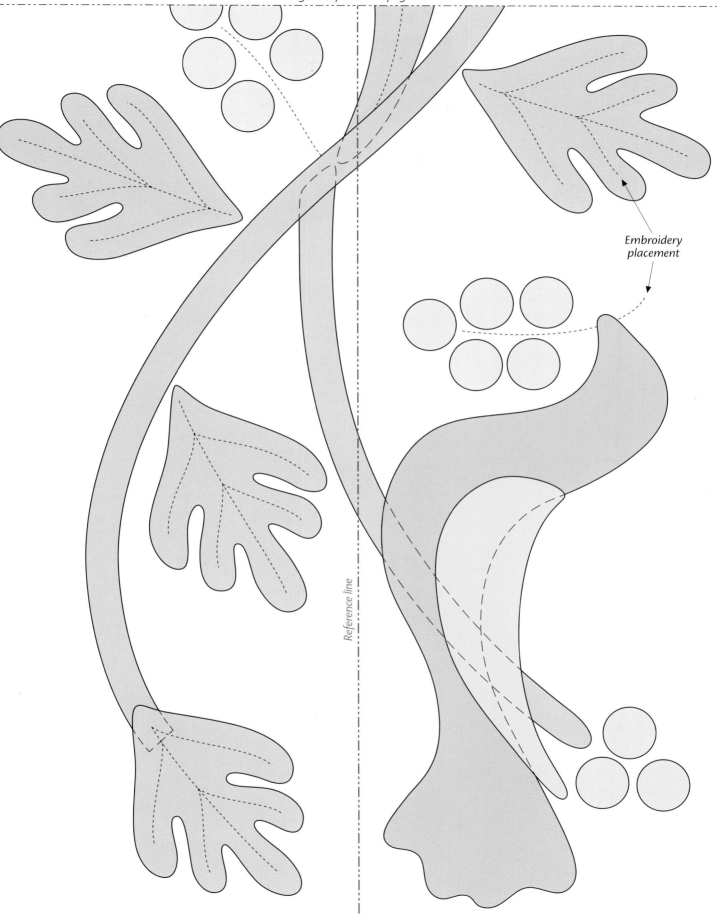

Embroidery
placement

Reference line

A SIMPLE LIFE

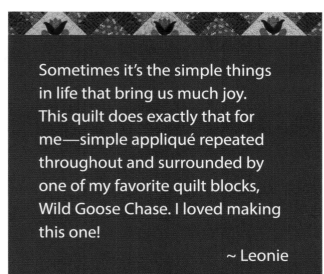

Sometimes it's the simple things in life that bring us much joy. This quilt does exactly that for me—simple appliqué repeated throughout and surrounded by one of my favorite quilt blocks, Wild Goose Chase. I loved making this one!

~ Leonie

FINISHED QUILT: 49½" x 49½"
FINISHED BLOCKS: 8¾" x 8¾"

"A Simple Life," designed, machine pieced, hand appliquéd, and machine quilted by Leonie Bateman

MATERIALS

Cotton Fabric

Yardage is based on 42"-wide fabric.

1½ yards of blue print for pieced blocks, setting triangles, and appliqué

1¼ yards of red print for pieced blocks and binding

⅝ yard of brown print for pieced blocks

⅜ yard *each* of 3 assorted light-tan prints for appliquéd-block backgrounds

3¼ yards of fabric for backing

Felted Wool Fabric

16" x 18" piece of claret for flowers

14" x 14" piece of green for stems and leaves

8" x 18" piece of teal for flowers

8" x 8" piece of cinnamon for flowers

Additional Materials

Embroidery floss in colors to match wool fabrics

58" x 58" piece of batting

40" length of freezer paper

Template plastic

Water-soluble glue stick

Appliqué glue

Stapler

CUTTING

From *each* of the 3 light-tan prints, cut:
3 squares, 9½" x 9½" (9 total)

From the brown print, cut:
7 strips, 2⅝" x 42"; crosscut into 96 squares, 2⅝" x 2⅝". Cut each square in half diagonally to yield a total of 192 triangles.

Continued on page 28

Continued from page 27

From the red print, cut:

7 strips, 2¼" x 42"; crosscut into 64 rectangles, 2¼" x 4"

3 strips, 2⅝" x 42"; crosscut into 32 squares, 2⅝" x 2⅝". Cut each square in half diagonally to yield a total of 64 triangles.

6 strips, 2¼" x 42"

From the blue print, cut:

4 strips, 4⅜" x 42"; crosscut into 32 squares, 4⅜" x 4⅜". Cut each square in half diagonally to yield 64 triangles.

1 strip, 2¼" x 42"; crosscut into 16 squares, 2¼" x 2¼"

1 strip, 14" x 42"; crosscut into 3 squares, 14" x 14". Cut each square into quarters diagonally to yield 12 side setting triangles.

1 strip, 7¼" x 42"; crosscut into 2 squares, 7¼" x 7¼". Cut each square in half diagonally to yield 4 corner setting triangles.

From the green wool, cut:

5 strips, ⅜" x 12"; crosscut into 36 stems, ⅜" x 1½"

PREPARING FOR APPLIQUÉ

1. Fold each light-tan 9½" square in half vertically and horizontally and finger-press the folds. Fold each square in half diagonally in both directions and finger-press the folds. If desired, mark over the fold lines with a water-soluble marker.

2. Refer to "Making a Master Pattern" (page 6) to make a master pattern using the patterns on page 30.

3. Refer to "Making the Appliqués" (page 6) to trace all of the appliqué shapes onto freezer paper, roughly cut out the shapes, and then iron the freezer-paper shapes onto your chosen colors of wool. Refer to the photo on page 26 and the materials list for fabric choices as needed. Cut out the wool shapes.

ADDING THE APPLIQUÉS

1. Refer to "Appliquéing Wool to the Background" (page 7) to position the four flower appliqués with stems and leaves on each of the background squares, working from the bottom layer to the top. Glue and staple your prepared appliqué pieces in place.

2. Using your thread and needle of choice, appliqué the pieces in place with a blanket stitch (page 8). Remove the staples.

3. Referring to "Needle-Turn Appliqué" (page 10), sew the large center circle to the appliquéd block and the small center circle onto the center flower.

4. Appliqué the center flower with the small circle onto the large circle.

5. Trim the blocks to 9¼" square, keeping the designs centered.

MAKING THE PIECED BLOCKS

1. Sew a red triangle and a brown triangle together to make a half-square-triangle unit. Press the seam allowances toward the brown triangle. Make a total of 64 half-square-triangle units.

Make 64.

2. Join a brown triangle to each red side of the half-square-triangle units as shown. Press the seam allowances toward the brown triangles.

3. Join a blue triangle to the pieced triangle unit from step 2 as shown. Press the seam allowances toward the blue triangle. Make a total of 64 units.

Make 64.

4. Arrange four of the units from step 3, four red 2¼" x 4" rectangles, and one blue 2¼" square into three rows as shown. Sew the units into rows and press the seam allowances toward the red rectangles. Sew the rows together and press the seam allowances toward the center row. Make 16 blocks.

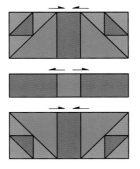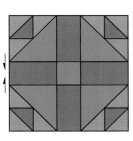

Make 16.

ASSEMBLING THE QUILT TOP

1. Arrange the pieced blocks, appliquéd blocks, and setting triangles into diagonal rows as shown. Sew the blocks and side setting triangles into diagonal rows. Press the seam allowances away from the pieced blocks. Sew the rows together, adding the corner setting triangles last. Press the seam allowances in one direction.

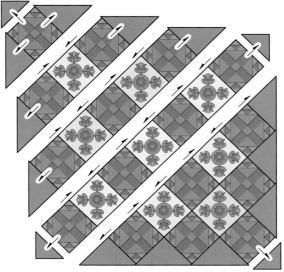

Quilt assembly

2. Trim and square up the quilt top, leaving a ¼" seam allowance beyond the corners of the blocks all the way around.

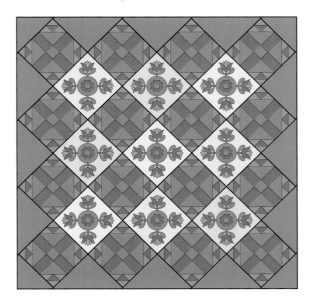

FINISHING

1. Cut and piece the backing fabric so it's 4" larger than the quilt top on each side. Sandwich the batting between the backing and quilt top, and baste the layers together.

2. Quilt as desired. Leonie quilted an allover design using her long-arm quilting machine.

3. Trim the backing and batting even with the quilt top. Refer to "Binding" (page 13) to bind the quilt edges with the red 2¼"-wide strips.

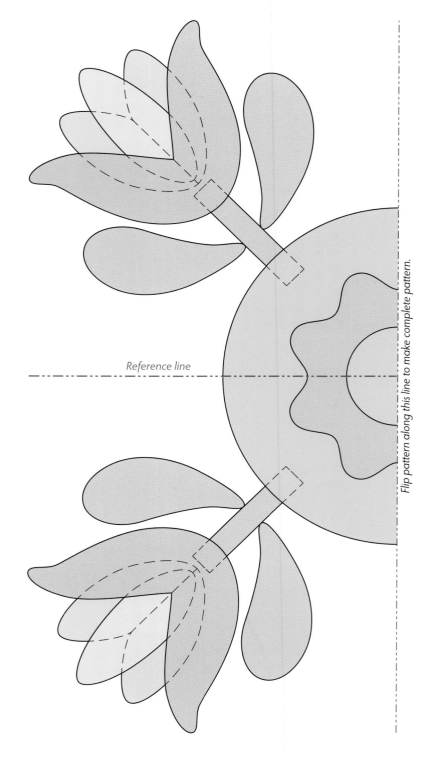

Reference line

Flip pattern along this line to make complete pattern.

Quilts with stars—one can never go past without stopping to admire them. And there are so many variations! For this quilt, I used 36 different fabrics to create a truly scrappy look. The center appliqué appears to float among the stars, which is how I feel when gazing at the stars in the night sky.

~ Leonie

FINISHED QUILT: 57¼" x 57¼"
FINISHED BLOCKS: 4½" x 4½"

"Dickinson," designed, machine pieced, hand appliquéd, and machine quilted by Leonie Bateman

MATERIALS

Cotton Fabric

Yardage is based on 42"-wide fabric.

3½ yards of shirting print for appliquéd-block background, pieced blocks, alternate blocks, and setting triangles

3" x 42" strip *each* of 36 assorted prints for the pieced blocks and reverse-appliqué inserts

⅝ yard of teal print for binding

3¾ yards of fabric for backing

Felted Wool Fabric

12" x 14" piece of brown for leaves and stems

10" x 12" piece of teal for flowers

10" x 12" piece of light-teal herringbone for flower sepals and center flower

5" x 8" of gingerbread plaid for pot

5" x 5" of cinnamon for bird bodies

3" x 4" of pomegranate for bird wings and tail

Additional Materials

Embroidery floss in colors to match wool fabrics

66" x 66" piece of batting

30" length of freezer paper

Water-soluble glue stick

Stapler

CUTTING

From the shirting print, cut:

1 strip, 21" x 42; from the strip cut:
   1 square, 21" x 21"
   72 squares, 2" x 2"

11 strips, 2¾" x 42"; crosscut into 144 squares, 2¾" x 2¾"

4 strips, 4½" x 42"; crosscut into 32 squares, 4½" x 4½"

4 strips, 8⅜" x 42"; crosscut into 16 squares, 8⅜" x 8⅜"; cut the squares into quarters diagonally to yield 64 side triangles

2 strips, 4¾" x 42"; crosscut into 16 squares, 4¾" x 4¾"; cut the squares in half diagonally to yield 32 corner triangles

Continued on page 33

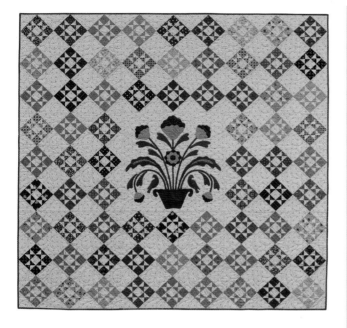

Continued from page 31

From *each* of the 36 assorted-print strips, cut:
4 squares, 2¾" x 2¾" (144 total)
8 squares, 2" x 2" (288 total)

From the teal print, cut:
7 strips, 2¼" x 42"

PREPARING FOR APPLIQUÉ

1. Fold the shirting-print 21" square in half vertically and horizontally and finger-press the folds. Fold the square in half diagonally in both directions and finger-press the folds. If desired, mark over the fold lines with a water-soluble marker.

2. Refer to "Making a Master Pattern" (page 6) to make a master pattern using the patterns on pages 35–37.

3. Refer to "Making the Appliqués" (page 6) to trace all of the appliqué shapes onto freezer paper, roughly cut out the shapes, and then iron the freezer-paper shapes onto your chosen colors of wool. Refer to the photo on page 32 and the materials list for fabric choices as needed. Cut out the wool shapes.

4. Refer to "Preassembling Units" (page 7) to assemble the center flower into a unit. Refer to "Reverse Appliqué" (page 9) to reverse appliqué the cutout sections of the leaves and flowers.

ADDING THE APPLIQUÉS

1. Refer to "Appliquéing Wool to the Background" (page 7) to position the appliqués on the background square, working from the bottom layer to the top. Glue and staple your prepared appliqué pieces in place.

2. Using your thread and needle of choice, appliqué the pieces in place with a blanket stitch (page 8). Remove the staples.

3. Trim the block to 19½" square, keeping the design centered.

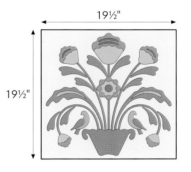

MAKING THE STAR BLOCKS

1. Referring to "Quarter-Square-Triangle Units" (page 12), mark a diagonal line from corner to corner in both directions on the wrong side of each of the shirting-print 2¾" squares. Place a marked square right sides together with an assorted-print square to make the quarter-square triangle units. Make 288 units.

Make 288.
(72 sets of 4 matching.)

2. Arrange four matching quarter-square triangle units, four matching 2" squares and one shirting-print 2" square into three horizontal rows as shown. Sew the pieces in each row together. Press the seam allowances toward the squares. Sew the rows together. Press the seam allowances toward the center. Make a total of 72 Star blocks.

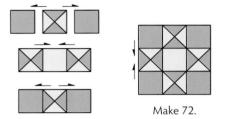

Make 72.

ASSEMBLING THE QUILT TOP

1. Arrange nine Star blocks, four shirting-print 4½" squares, eight side triangles and four corner triangles into diagonal rows as shown. Sew the pieces in each row together. Press the seam allowances toward the shirting-print squares. Sew the rows together, adding the corner triangles last. Trim the section, leaving a ¼" seam allowance beyond the block corners all the way around. Make a total of eight Star block sections.

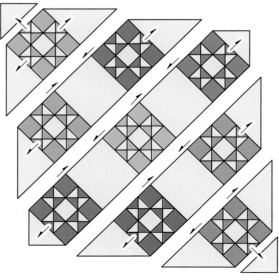

Make 8.

2. Arrange the block sections and the center appliquéd block into three horizontal rows as shown. Sew the sections in each row together. Press the seam allowances as shown. Sew the rows together. Press the seam allowances toward the center row.

Quilt assembly

FINISHING

1. Cut and piece the backing fabric so it's 4" larger than the quilt top on each side. Sandwich the batting between the backing and quilt top, and baste the layers together.

2. Quilt as desired. Leonie quilted an allover design using her long-arm quilting machine.

3. Trim the backing and batting even with the quilt top. Refer to "Binding" (page 13) to bind the quilt edges with the teal 2¼"-wide strips.

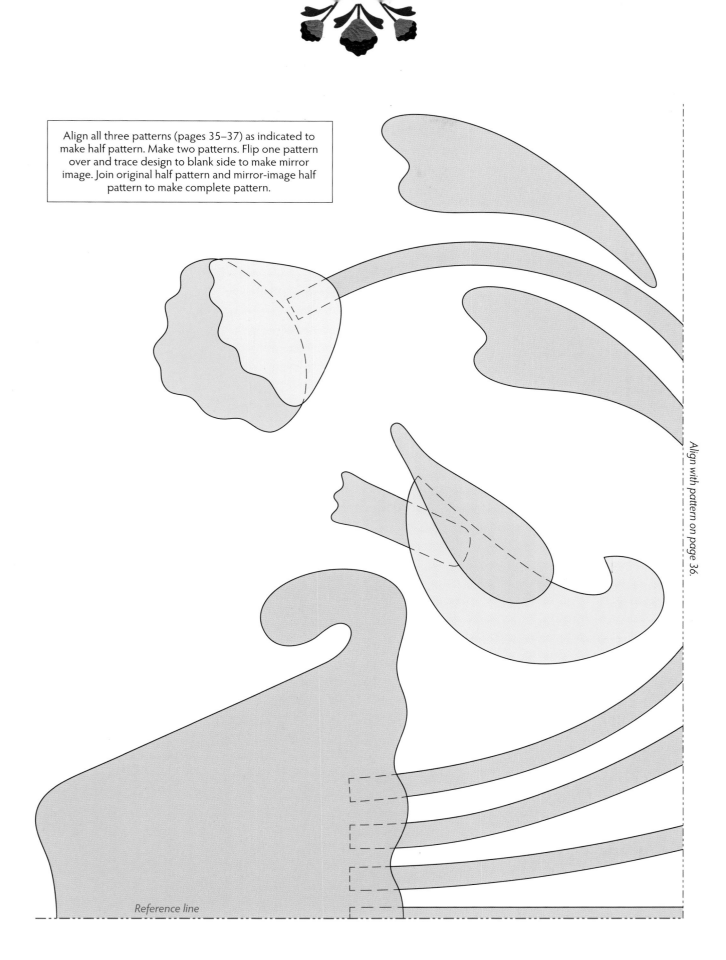

Align all three patterns (pages 35–37) as indicated to make half pattern. Make two patterns. Flip one pattern over and trace design to blank side to make mirror image. Join original half pattern and mirror-image half pattern to make complete pattern.

Reference line

Align with pattern on page 36.

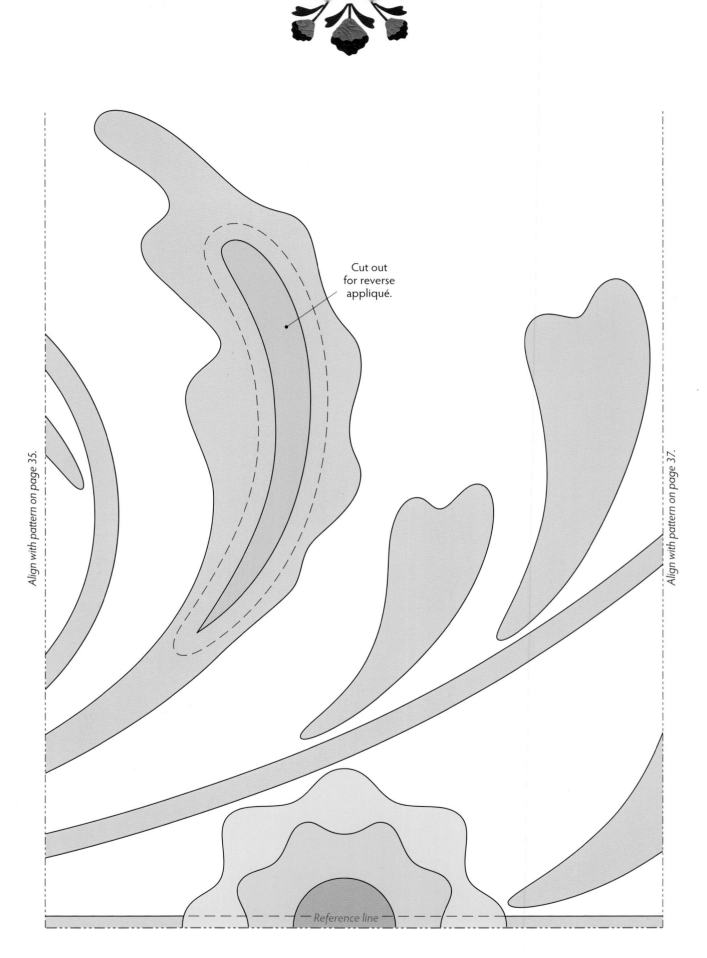

Cut out
for reverse
appliqué.

Align with pattern on page 35.

Align with pattern on page 37.

Reference line

Country Elegance

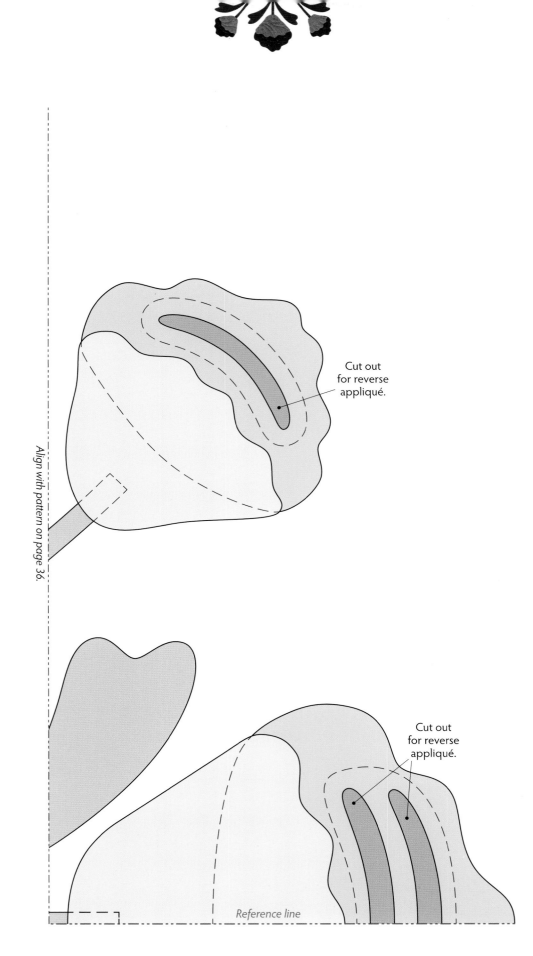

Cut out
for reverse
appliqué.

Align with pattern on page 36.

Cut out
for reverse
appliqué.

Reference line

Dickinson

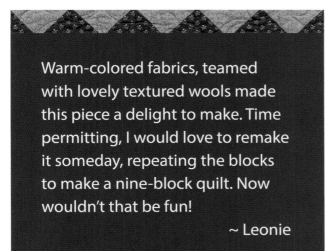

Warm-colored fabrics, teamed with lovely textured wools made this piece a delight to make. Time permitting, I would love to remake it someday, repeating the blocks to make a nine-block quilt. Now wouldn't that be fun!

~ Leonie

FINISHED QUILT: 28" x 28"

"Hampden Lane," designed, machine pieced, hand appliquéd, and hand and machine quilted by Leonie Bateman

MATERIALS

Cotton Fabric

Yardage is based on 42"-wide fabric.

1 yard of charcoal print for background, Four Patch blocks, and binding

⅓ yard of blue print for pieced border

⅓ yard of light-olive print for pieced border

¼ yard of rust print for inner border and Four Patch blocks

1 yard of fabric for backing

Felted Wool Fabric

12" x 20" piece of teal for large and small flowers and small center circle

12" x 20" piece of light olive for reverse-appliqué inserts, tips of small flowers and large center circle

5" x 14" piece of rust for center leaves and flower bases

5" x 8" piece of medium purple for stems

Additional Materials

Embroidery floss in colors to match wool fabrics

36" x 36" piece of batting

20" length of freezer paper

Water-soluble glue stick

Stapler

CUTTING

From the charcoal print, cut:
1 square, 22½" x 22½"

1 strip, 1½" x 14"

4 strips, 2¼" x 42"

From the rust print, cut:
4 strips, 1½" x 42"; crosscut into:

    2 strips, 1½" x 22½"

    2 strips, 1½" x 24½"

    1 strip, 1½" x 14"

From the light-olive print, cut:
3 strips, 2½" x 42"; crosscut into 48 squares, 2½" x 2½"

From the blue print, cut:
3 strips, 2½" x 42"; crosscut into 24 rectangles, 2½" x 4½"

From the medium-purple wool, cut:
4 stems, ⅜" x 5½"

8 stems, ⅜" x 7"

PIECING THE QUILT TOP

1. Sew a rust 1½" x 22½" strip to each side of the charcoal 22½" center square. Press the seam allowances toward the center square. Sew rust 1½" x 24½" strips to the top and bottom of the center square. Press the seam allowances toward the center square.

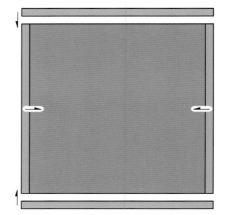

2. Mark a diagonal line from corner to corner on the wrong side of each of the light-olive 2½" squares. Referring to "Quick Corner Triangles" (page 11), place marked squares on opposite ends of a blue 2½" x 4½" rectangle, right sides together. Sew on the marked lines. Trim the seam allowances to ¼". Press the triangles toward the corners. Make 24 flying-geese units.

Make 24.

3. Sew six flying-geese units together along the short edges, with the points going in the same direction, as shown, to make a border strip. Press the seam allowances in one direction. Make a total of four border strips.

Make 4.

4. Join a rust 1½" x 14" strip and a charcoal 1½" x 14" strip along the long edges to make a strip set. Press the seam allowances toward the charcoal strip. Crosscut the strip set into eight segments, 1½" wide.

1½"

5. Join two segments from step 4 as shown to make a four-patch unit. Make four units.

Make 4.

6. Sew a flying-geese border strip to each side of the quilt center. Press the seam allowances toward the rust strips. Sew a four-patch unit to each end of the remaining two flying-geese border strips as shown. Press the seam allowances toward the four-patch units. Join

these strips to the top and bottom of the quilt. Press the seam allowances toward the rust strips.

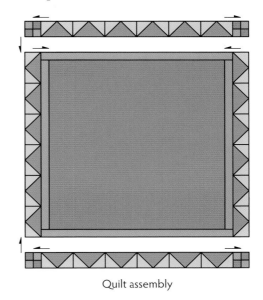

Quilt assembly

PREPARING FOR APPLIQUÉ

1. Fold the quilt top in half vertically and horizontally and finger-press the folds. Fold the quilt top in half diagonally in each direction and finger-press the folds. Use a white pencil or other marking tool of your choice to mark over the folds. Because you're working with a dark background fabric, these lines will be used as guidelines to help position the appliqués.

2. Refer to "Making a Master Pattern" (page 6) to make a master pattern using the quarter pattern on pages 42 and 43. You'll need to trace the quarter pattern four times, and then join the pieces to make the complete pattern.

3. Refer to "Making the Appliqués" (page 6) to trace all of the appliqué shapes onto freezer paper, roughly cut out the shapes, and then iron the freezer-paper shapes onto your chosen colors of wool. Refer to the photo on page 38 and the materials list for fabric choices as needed. Cut out the wool shapes.

4. Refer to "Preassembling Units" (page 7) to assemble the center circle pieces into a unit.

5. Refer to "Reverse Appliqué" (page 9) to reverse appliqué the cutout sections of the large and small flowers.

ADDING THE APPLIQUÉS

1. Refer to "Appliquéing Wool to the Background" (page 7) to position the appliqués on the background fabric, working from the bottom layer to the top. Because you're working with a dark background fabric, use the marked reference lines on your background to help you place the appliqués. Glue and staple your prepared appliqué pieces in place.

2. Using your thread and needle of choice, appliqué the pieces in place with a blanket stitch (page 8). Remove the staples.

FINISHING

1. Cut the backing fabric so it's 4" larger than the quilt top on each side. Sandwich the batting between the backing and quilt top, and baste the layers together.

2. Quilt as desired. Leonie machine quilted large and small feathers around the appliqués and added some hand quilting stitches inside the appliqués.

3. Trim the backing and batting even with the quilt top. Refer to "Binding" (page 13) to bind the quilt edges with the charcoal 2¼"-wide strips.

> Align patterns as indicated to make a quarter pattern. Make four quarter patterns, and then join pieces to make complete pattern.

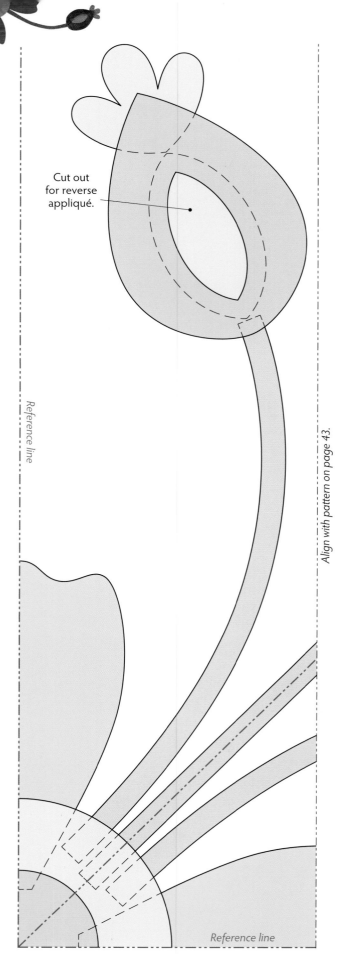

Cut out for reverse appliqué.

Reference line

Align with pattern on page 43.

Reference line

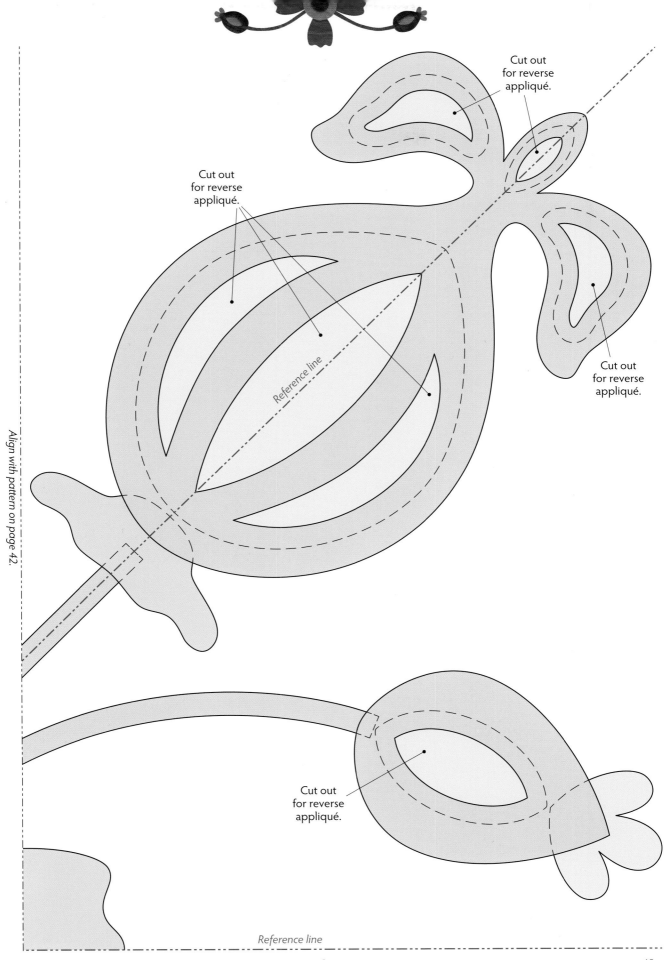

Cut out
for reverse
appliqué.

Cut out
for reverse
appliqué.

Cut out
for reverse
appliqué.

Reference line

Align with pattern on page 42.

Cut out
for reverse
appliqué.

Reference line

MANGAL'S VISIT

Who can pass up lovely appliqué in a wooden frame? I know I can't! Framed pieces look beautiful on the wall of your home and create a warm feel. One can never have too many! "Mangal's Visit" evokes fond memories of my dear friend from childhood who was visiting at the time I was working on this piece.

~ Leonie

UNFRAMED FINISHED PIECE: 10" x 20"

"Mangal's Visit," designed, hand appliquéd, and hand quilted by Leonie Bateman

MATERIALS

Cotton Fabric

Yardage is based on 42"-wide fabric.

⅜ yard of gold floral for background*

A fat quarter will work if it's at least 22" wide.

Felted Wool Fabric

4" x 24" piece of sea green for dogtooth border

7" x 12" piece of sea green for stems and leaves

4" x 9" piece of brown herringbone for pot

6" x 12" piece of claret for large flower and small flowers

4" x 6" piece of antique gold for small flowers

6" x 12" piece of cinnamon for base of large flower and reverse-appliqué inserts for leaves and large flower

3" x 3" piece of blue for small-flower reverse-appliqué inserts

Additional Materials

Embroidery floss in colors to match wool fabrics

24" length of freezer paper

Water-soluble glue stick

Stapler

10" x 20" purchased frame (The opening should be at least 9½" x 19½".)

CUTTING

From the gold floral, cut:

1 rectangle, 12" x 22"

From the sea-green wool, cut:

2 strips, ⅜" x 24"; crosscut into:

    1 stem, ⅜" x 12"

    2 stems, ⅜" x 7"

    2 stems, ⅜" x 4"

PREPARING FOR APPLIQUÉ

1. Fold the piece of gold floral in half vertically and horizontally; finger-press the folds.

2. Measure the length and width of the front opening of your frame. Center and mark the opening measurements on your background fabric, keeping the rectangle centered. The easiest way to do this is to first calculate half of the length. Find this measurement on your acrylic ruler and position that line on the horizontal fold line of the background fabric; mark across the top of the ruler. Continue across the horizontal line to mark the entire length across the top of the fabric. Repeat to measure and mark across the bottom of the fabric.

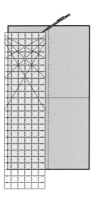

3. In the same manner, calculate half the width of the opening, measure from the vertical fold line, and mark down the sides of the background fabric. These will be the guidelines for placing the dogtooth border appliqué pieces.

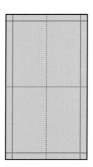

4. Refer to "Cutting the Border Strips" (page 8) to trace the dogtooth border pattern on page 49 onto freezer paper, repeating the design to make a strip 22" long for a side border. Repeat to make one additional side border strip. In the same manner, make an additional border strip measuring 24", which you will cut in half to use for the top and bottom border strips. These strips will measure 12". Use the freezer-paper patterns to cut the dogtooth border strips from the sea-green wool.

ADDING THE APPLIQUÉS

1. Refer to "Positioning the Border Strips" (page 9) to place the dogtooth border strips on the background fabric, making sure to align the inner points with the marked lines on the background. Glue and staple the borders in place.

2. Refer to "Making a Master Pattern" (page 6) to make a master pattern using the patterns on pages 47–49.

3. Refer to "Making the Appliqués" (page 6) to trace all of the appliqué shapes onto freezer paper, roughly cut out the shapes, and then iron the freezer-paper shapes onto your chosen colors of wool. Refer to the photo on page 44 and the materials list for fabric choices as needed. Cut out the wool shapes.

4. Refer to "Reverse Appliqué" (page 9) to reverse appliqué the cutout sections of the large flower, small flowers, and leaves.

5. Lay your master pattern on a light box or other light source, and then position the prepared background fabric on top of the master pattern, lining up the center folds of the background with the reference lines on the master pattern. Pin the background to the master pattern.

6. Refer to "Appliquéing Wool to the Background" (page 7) to glue and staple your prepared appliqué pieces in place, working from the bottom layer to the top.

7. Using your thread and needle of choice, appliqué pieces in place with a blanket stitch (page 8). Remove the staples.

FINISHING

To complete this project, Leonie marked a diagonal crosshatch design with the lines spaced ½" apart through the pot using a ruler and white pencil. She then hand quilted the lines. She did the same to the base of the large flower, with the lines spaced ¼" apart. This quilting creates a nice texture while anchoring the pieces to the background. Insert the quilted piece into purchased frame, or bind if desired.

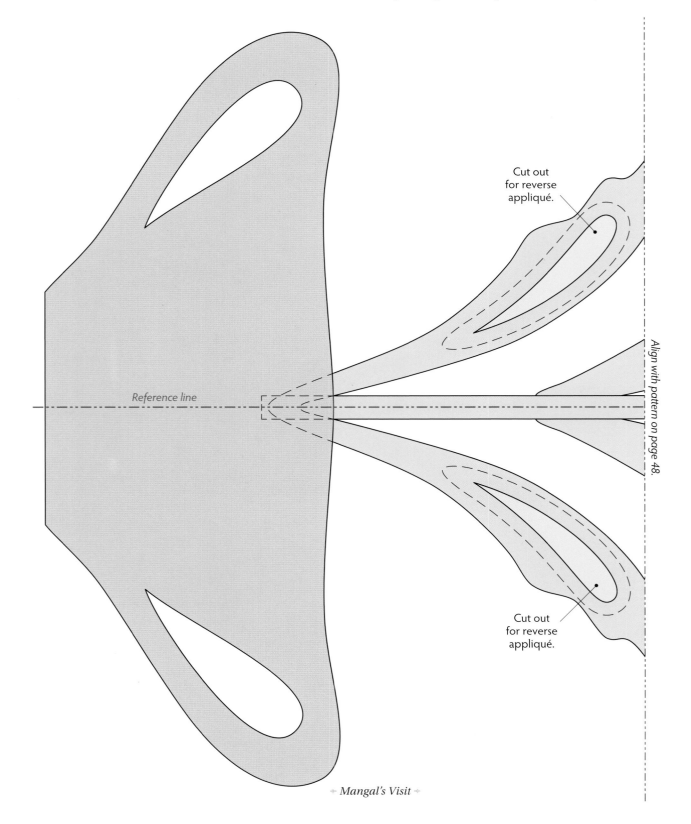

Cut out
for reverse
appliqué.

Reference line

Align with pattern on page 48.

Cut out
for reverse
appliqué.

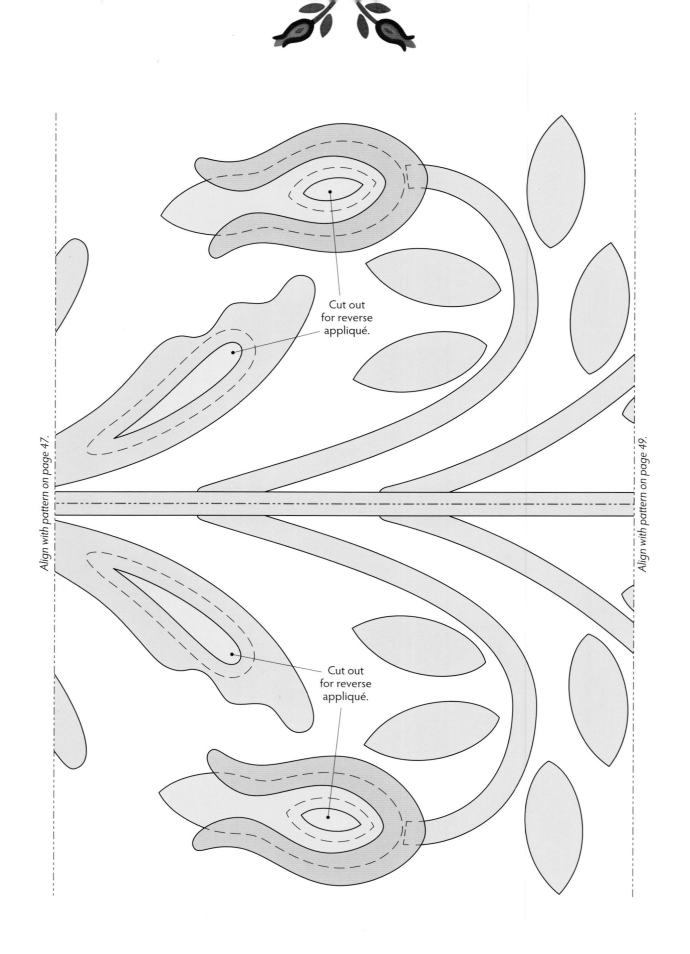

Cut out for reverse appliqué.

Cut out for reverse appliqué.

Align with pattern on page 47.

Align with pattern on page 49.

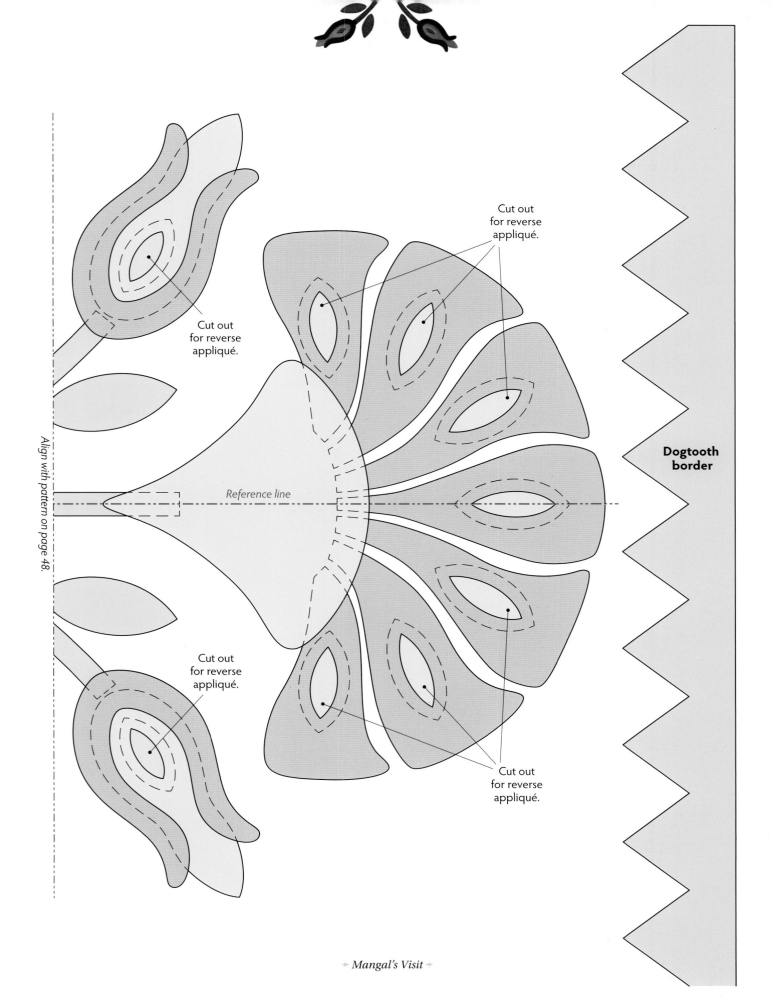

Cut out
for reverse
appliqué.

Cut out
for reverse
appliqué.

Cut out
for reverse
appliqué.

Cut out
for reverse
appliqué.

Reference line

Align with pattern on page 48.

**Dogtooth
border**

HEARTS AND FLOWERS

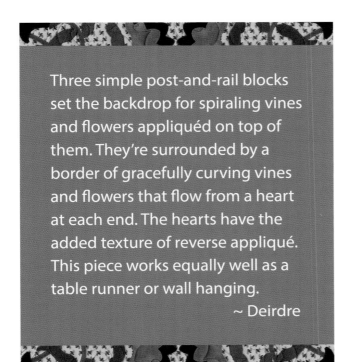

Three simple post-and-rail blocks set the backdrop for spiraling vines and flowers appliquéd on top of them. They're surrounded by a border of gracefully curving vines and flowers that flow from a heart at each end. The hearts have the added texture of reverse appliqué. This piece works equally well as a table runner or wall hanging.

~ Deirdre

FINISHED QUILT: 22" x 42"
FINISHED BLOCKS: 10" x 10"

"Hearts and Flowers," designed, machine pieced, hand appliquéd, and machine quilted by Deirdre Bond-Abel

MATERIALS

Cotton Fabric

Yardage is based on 42"-wide fabric.

⅞ yard of cream print for border

⅛ yard *each* of 3 dark prints and 2 light prints for pieced blocks

5" x 10" scrap of light-blue print for reverse-appliqué inserts

⅜ yard of tan print for binding

1½ yards of fabric for backing

Felted Wool Fabric

5" x 48" piece of teal for leaves and flower sepals

5" x 24" piece of dark red for flowers

3" x 48" piece of dusty pink for flowers

3" x 48" piece of mushroom brown for stems

5" x 10" piece of mottled red for hearts

Additional Materials

Embroidery floss in colors to match wool fabrics

30" x 50" piece of batting

36" length of freezer paper

Water-soluble glue stick

Stapler

CUTTING

From *each* of the 3 dark and 2 light prints, cut:

2 strips, 1½" x 42" (6 dark, 4 light total)

From the cream print, cut:

2 strips, 6½" x 22½"

2 strips, 6½" x 30½"

From the tan print, cut:

4 strips, 2¼" x 42"

From the light-blue print, cut:

2 squares, 5" x 5"

From the mushroom-brown wool, cut:

7 strips, ¼" x 48"; crosscut into:

    4 stems, ¼" x 25"

    4 stems, ¼" x 11"

    4 stems, ¼" x 5"

    6 stems, ¼" x 18"

MAKING THE POST-AND-RAIL BLOCKS

1. Arrange a 1½" x 42" strip from each print so the darkest and lightest prints are on the outside edges. Sew the strips together along their long edges and press the seam allowances in one direction. Make two identical strip sets. Crosscut the strip sets into 12 segments, 5½" wide.

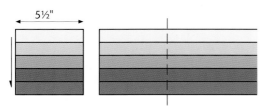

Make 2 strip sets.
Cut 12 segments.

2. Arrange four segments together, rotating the segments as shown and keeping the dark prints toward the center. Sew two segments together in pairs and press the seam allowances in opposite directions. Sew the two halves together to make one block and press the seam allowances in one direction. Make three blocks.

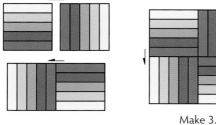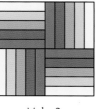

Make 3.

3. Stay-stitch ⅛" from the edges of each block to stabilize the seams and prevent raveling while you are working with them.

BLOCK APPLIQUÉ

Appliqué each block before sewing them together for easier handling.

1. Refer to "Making a Master Pattern" (page 6) to make a master pattern for the block appliqué using the block pattern on page 54.

2. Refer to "Making the Appliqués" (page 6) to trace all of the appliqué shapes onto freezer paper. Roughly cut out the shapes, and then iron the freezer-paper shapes onto the chosen colors of wool. Refer to the photo on page 50 and the materials list for fabric choices as needed. Cut out the wool shapes.

3. Lay the master pattern on a light box or other light source, and then position a block on top of the master pattern, lining up the seam lines with the reference lines on the pattern. Pin the block to the master pattern.

4. Refer to "Appliquéing Wool to the Background" (page 7) to glue and staple your prepared appliqué pieces in place. Use the mushroom-brown ¼" x 18" strips for the stems. Add glue to one strip and then press it into place following the outline of the master pattern underneath the block. Add the second strip crossing it over the first in the middle of the block. Add the two flower segments to each end of the strips, and then add the leaves last.

5. Appliqué the pieces in place using a blanket stitch (page 8). Remove the staples. Repeat for all three blocks.

6. Sew the three blocks together and press the seam allowances in one direction.

ADDING THE BORDERS

1. Sew the cream 6½" x 30½" border strips to the long sides of the quilt center and press the seam allowances toward the border strips.

2. Sew the cream 6½" x 22½" border strips to the short ends of the quilt center and press the seam allowances toward the border strips.

BORDER APPLIQUÉ

1. Refer to "Reverse Appliqué" (page 9) and "Making the Appliqués" to prepare and stitch the reverse appliqué for the two red wool hearts using the light-blue 5" squares.

2. Refer to "Making a Master Pattern" to make a master pattern for one quarter of the border appliqué design using the patterns on pages 55–57.

3. Refer to "Making the Appliqués" to trace all of the appliqué shapes onto freezer paper. Roughly cut out the shapes, and then iron the freezer-paper shapes onto your chosen colors of wool. Refer to the photo on page 50 and the materials list for fabric choices as needed. Cut out the wool shapes.

4. Lay the master pattern on a light box or other light source, and then position the pieced quilt over the top of the master pattern, lining up the side seam lines with the reference lines on the master pattern, and pin the quilt to the master pattern.

5. Refer to "Appliquéing Wool to the Background" to glue and staple your prepared pieces in place. Begin with one of the mushroom-brown ¼" x 11" strips, add glue, and press the strip into place following the outline of the master pattern underneath the fabric.

6. Add the mushroom-brown ¼" x 25" strip, starting from where the strip sits underneath the leaf that comes out of the heart shape, and then curve it around and up, pressing it into place following the pattern outline.

7. Add the ¼" x 5" stems that come out from under the end leaves, the flower segments, and then the leaves.

8. Unpin the quilt from the master pattern. Turn the master pattern over and trace the outline of the appliqué through to the other side to make a mirror image.

9. Reposition the other side of the quilt over the master pattern, again lining up the side seams with the reference lines on the master pattern. Pin the quilt to the master pattern.

10. Position the appliqué shapes in the same order as the first side.

11. Add the prepared heart shape to the middle of the end border.

12. Unpin the quilt and turn it around, repositioning it over the master pattern, and then add the remaining appliqué shapes to that end of the quilt.

13. Appliqué the pieces in place using a blanket stitch. Remove the staples.

FINISHING

1. Cut the backing fabric so it's 4" larger than the quilt top on each side. Sandwich the batting between the backing and the quilt top, and baste the layers together.

2. Quilt as desired. Deirdre machine quilted an allover swirling design.

3. Trim the backing and batting even with the quilt top. Refer to "Binding" (page 13) to bind the quilt edges with the tan 2¼"-wide strips.

Make two patterns. Rotate one pattern 180°
and join patterns to make complete pattern.

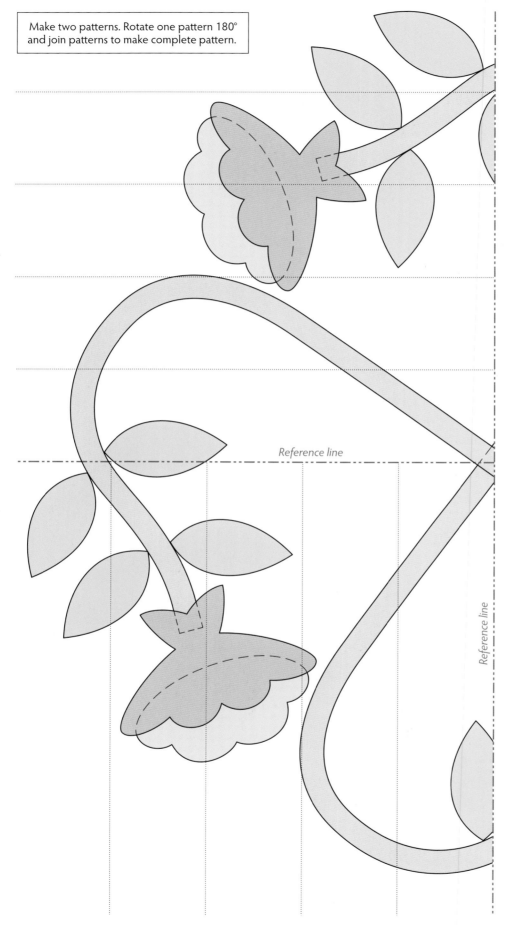

Reference line

Reference line

Align the three patterns (pages 55–57) as indicated to make half pattern. Make two patterns. Flip one pattern over and trace design to make mirror image. Join original half pattern and mirror-image half pattern to make complete pattern.

Cut out for reverse appliqué.

Reference line

Side border seam

Appliqué placement diagram

Align with pattern on page 56.

Side border seam

Reference line

Align with pattern on page 57.

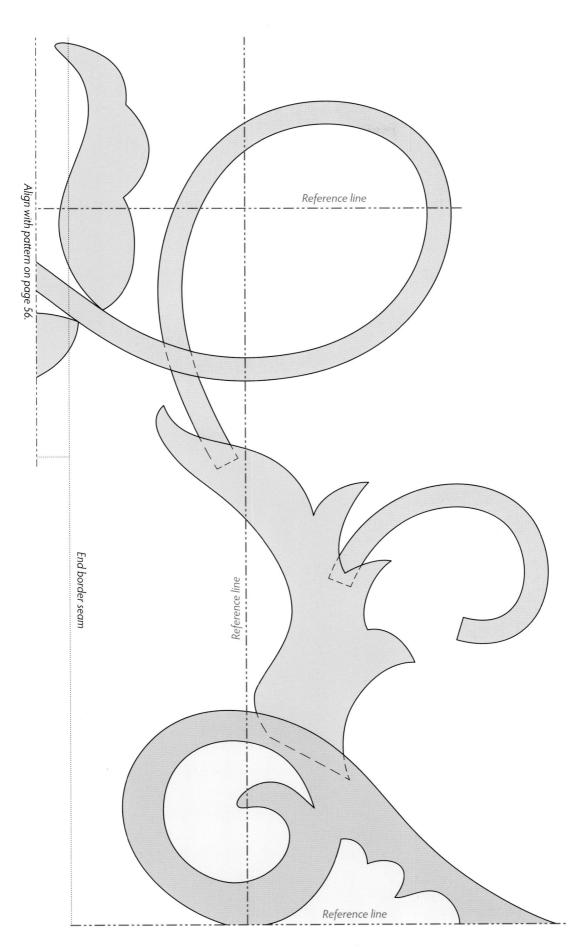

Align with pattern on page 56.

End border seam

Reference line

Reference line

Reference line

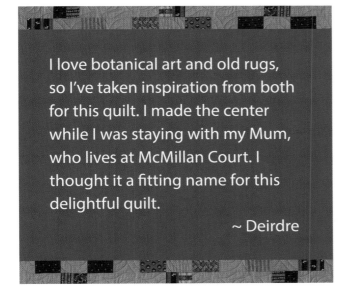

I love botanical art and old rugs, so I've taken inspiration from both for this quilt. I made the center while I was staying with my Mum, who lives at McMillan Court. I thought it a fitting name for this delightful quilt.

~ Deirdre

FINISHED QUILT: 60" x 76"

"McMillan Court," designed, machine pieced, hand appliquéd, and machine quilted by Deirdre Bond-Abel

MATERIALS

Cotton Fabric

Yardage is based on 42- wide fabric.

4 yards of light-bronze print for appliquéd-block backgrounds and pieced blocks

¼ yard *each* of 12 assorted medium to dark prints for pieced bocks

⅝ yard of dark-red print for binding

4 yards of fabric for backing

Felted Wool Fabric

8" x 12" piece of burgundy for flower 1A

6" x 6" piece of lime green for flower 1B

4" x 6" piece of dark purple for flower 2A

6" x 8" piece of mauve for flower 2B

6" x 6" piece of light tan for flower 2C

6" x 8" piece of green for flower 3A

4" x 6" piece of mustard for flower 3B

6" x 12" piece of medium purple for flower 3C

10" x 20" piece of dusty pink for flower 4A

2" x 4" piece of light-pink herringbone for flower 4B

8" x 12" piece of dark-pink herringbone for flower 5A

6" x 8" piece of dusty pink for flower 5B

6" x 20" piece of green for leaf 1

5" x 24" piece of copper for leaf 2

8" x 20" piece of mottled brown for leaves 3A, 3B, and 3C

14" x 20" piece of mottled dark green for leaf 4

12" x 16" piece of medium green for leaf 5

14" x 18" piece of gold for stem base

8" x 12" piece of green for stems

Additional Materials

Embroidery floss in colors to match wool fabrics

68" x 84" piece of batting

72" length of freezer paper

Water-soluble glue stick

Stapler

CUTTING

From the light-bronze print, cut:

1 rectangle, 25" x 33"

4 rectangles, 13" x 17"

30 strips, 2½" x 42"; crosscut into:

   8 rectangles, 2½" x 12½"

   40 rectangles, 2½" x 8½"

   32 rectangles, 2½" x 6½"

   72 rectangles, 2½" x 4½"

   72 squares, 2½" x 2½"

Continued on page 60

Continued from page 59

From *each* of the 12 assorted prints, cut:

1 strip, 2½" x 42"; crosscut into 12 squares,
    2½" x 2½" (144 total; 4 will be extra)

4 rectangles, 2½" x 4½" (48 total)

From the 8" x 12" piece of green wool, cut:

24 strips, ¼" x 12"; from these, cut:

    16 stems, ¼" x 10"

    8 stems, ¼" x 8"

    8 stems, ¼" x 3½"

    8 stems, ¼" x 1¼"

From the dark-red print, cut:

8 strips, 2¼" x 42"

PREPARING FOR APPLIQUÉ

1. Fold the light-bronze 25" x 33" rectangle for the center block in half vertically and horizontally and finger-press the folds. If desired, mark over the fold lines with a water-soluble marker.

2. Fold each of the light-bronze 13" x 17" rectangles for the corner blocks in half vertically and horizontally and mark lines in the same manner.

3. Refer to "Making a Master Pattern" (page 6) to make a master pattern using the patterns on pages 63–66.

4. Refer to "Making the Appliqués" (page 6) to trace all of the appliqué shapes for each block onto freezer paper, roughly cut out the shapes, and then iron the freezer-paper shapes onto your chosen colors of wool. You will need four sets of appliqué shapes for the center block and four sets for the corner blocks. Refer to the photo on page 58 and the materials list for color choices as needed. Cut out the wool shapes.

ADDING THE APPLIQUÉS

1. Refer to "Appliquéing Wool to the Background" (page 7) to position the appliqués on each of the background pieces.

2. You will position the appliqués for the center block one quarter at a time. Position one quarter of the background fabric over the master pattern and line up the fold lines with the reference lines on the master pattern. Pin the two together and place over a light source.

3. Starting with the stems, glue the pieces in place, and then add the flower segments working from the bottom up. Add the leaves and the gold stem base last.

4. Unpin the fabric from the master pattern. Turn the master pattern over and trace the outline of the appliqué through to the other side to make a mirror image. Reposition the fabric over the mirror-image pattern and add the appliqués for the next quarter.

5. Reposition the fabric and the pattern and add the remaining two quarters. Once you're happy with the placement, staple the appliqués in place.

6. Position appliqués in the corner blocks in the same way, making sure two are right facing and two are left facing.

7. Using your thread and needle of choice, appliqué the pieces in place with a blanket stitch (page 8). Remove the staples.

8. Trim the center block to measure 24½" x 32½" and each of the corner blocks to measure 12½" x 16½".

MAKING THE PIECED BLOCKS

The pieced blocks are arranged in a "Barn Raising" layout between and around the appliquéd blocks. Place the assorted medium to dark squares and rectangles randomly when piecing to give the quilt a nice scrappy look.

1. Arrange ten assorted 2½" squares and two assorted 2½" x 4½" rectangles with the following pieces cut from light-bronze print: four squares, 2½" x 2½"; four rectangles, 2½" x 4½"; two rectangles, 2½" x 6½"; and four rectangles, 2½" x 8½". Sew the pieces into rows and press the seam allowances toward the assorted prints. Sew the rows together and press the seam allowances in one direction. Make four blocks.

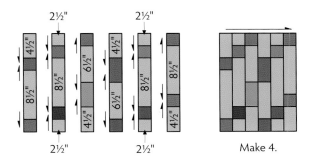

Make 4.

2. Repeat step 1, but arrange the pieces as shown so that the diagonal pattern made by the assorted prints is going in the opposite direction. Make four blocks.

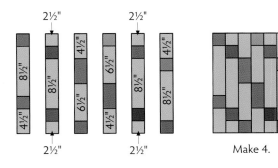

Make 4.

3. Arrange two assorted 2½" squares and three assorted 2½" x 4½" rectangles with the following pieces cut from light-bronze print: two squares, 2½" x 2½"; one rectangle, 2½" x 4½"; two rectangles, 2½" x 6½"; and one rectangle, 2½" x 12½". Sew the pieces into rows and press the seam allowances toward the assorted prints. Sew the rows together and press the seam allowances in one direction. Make eight blocks for the sides.

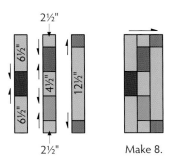

Make 8.

4. Arrange four assorted 2½" squares and one assorted 2½" x 4½" rectangle with the following pieces cut from light-bronze print: two squares, 2½" x 2½"; three rectangles, 2½" x 4½"; and one rectangle, 2½" x 8½". Sew the pieces into rows and press the seam allowances toward the assorted prints. Sew the rows together and press the seam allowances in one direction. Make eight blocks for the top and bottom.

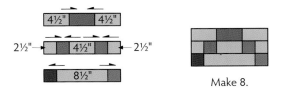

Make 8.

5. Arrange three assorted 2½" squares, two light-bronze 2½" squares, and two light-bronze 2½" x 4½" rectangles as shown. Sew the pieces into rows and press the seam allowances toward the assorted prints. Sew the rows together and

press the seam allowances in one direction. Make two of each block for the corners.

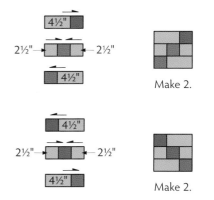

Make 2.

Make 2.

ASSEMBLING THE QUILT TOP

1. Arrange all of the pieced and appliquéd blocks into rows as shown. Sew the blocks into rows, making sure that the appliqué and the piecing are all facing in the correct direction. Press the seam allowances as shown.

2. Sew the rows together and press the seam allowances toward the least bulky side to complete your quilt top.

Quilt assembly

FINISHING

1. Cut and piece the backing fabric so it's 4" larger than the quilt top on each side. Sandwich the batting between the backing and the quilt top. Baste the layers together.

2. Quilt as desired. Deirdre machine quilted an allover design.

3. Trim the backing and batting even with the quilt top.

4. Refer to "Binding" (page 13) to bind the quilt edges with the dark-red 2¼"-wide strips.

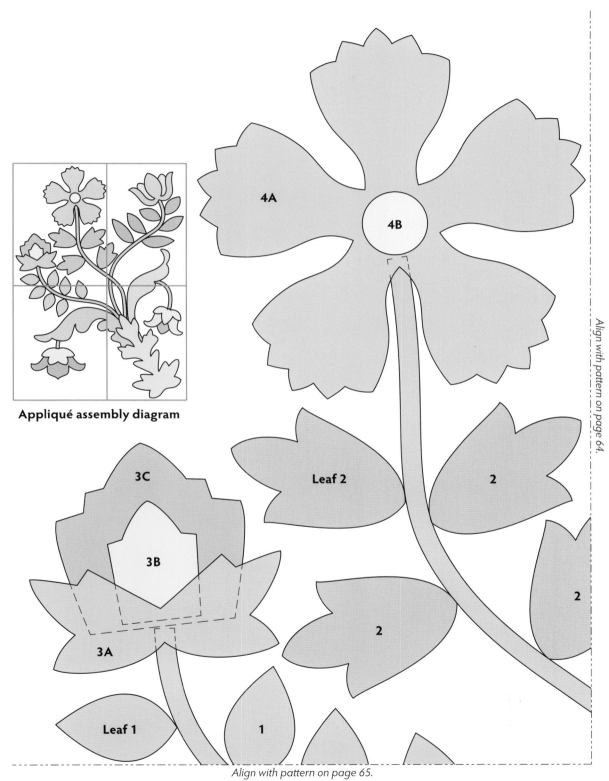

Appliqué assembly diagram

4A

4B

3C

3B

3A

Leaf 2

2

2

2

Leaf 1

1

Align with pattern on page 64.

Align with pattern on page 65.

Align with pattern on page 63.

5B

5A

3A

Leaf 3A

3B

3B

3C

3C

Align with pattern on page 66.

Align with pattern on page 63.

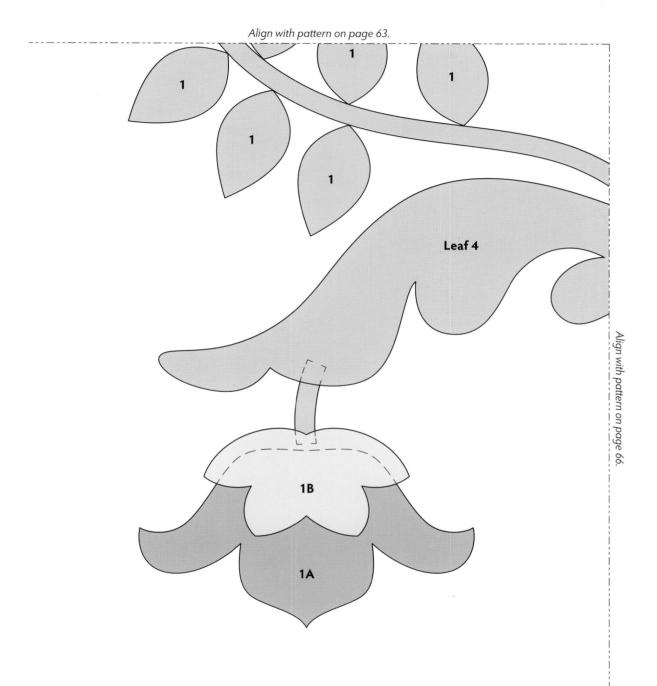

1

1

1

1

1

Leaf 4

1B

1A

Align with pattern on page 66.

Align with pattern on page 64.

Leaf 5

2C

2B

2A

Align with pattern on page 65.

Stem base

WYNYARD

Tulips are definitely my favorite flower to appliqué—I love their symmetry. When deciding on pieced blocks to go with the appliqué, I like to continue the shapes from the appliqué. In this quilt, the tulips form a diagonal cross, so I chose pieced blocks that echo the cross formation. Wynyard is a town in the north of our state, famous for growing tulips. I thought that was the perfect name for this quilt. I love the bright colors of these reproduction prints. Several antique quilts in my collection are made from the original prints they are based on, making them dear to my heart.

~ Deirdre

FINISHED QUILT: 48" x 48"
FINISHED BLOCKS: 16" x 16"

"Wynyard," designed, machine pieced, hand appliquéd, and machine quilted by Deirdre Bond-Abel

MATERIALS

Cotton Fabric

Yardage is based on 42"-wide fabric.

1⅛ yards of cream print for appliquéd-block backgrounds

⅔ yard of blue print for pieced blocks

½ yard of yellow print for pieced blocks

½ yard of green print for pieced blocks

½ yard of red print for pieced blocks*

½ yard of red print for binding*

3¼ yards of fabric for backing

Felted Wool Fabric

Yardage is based on 48"-wide fabric.

⅓ yard of green herringbone for curved stems

12" x 24" piece of gold houndstooth for center motif

12" x 24" piece of mustard for center motif

10" x 24" piece of gold for tulips and center circle

10" x 12" piece of rust for tulips

10" x 12" piece of cherry red for flowers, buds, and center circle

6" x 8" piece of teal herringbone for flowers

5" x 8" piece of green for straight stems

Additional Materials

Embroidery floss in colors to match wool fabrics

56" x 56" piece of batting

72" length of freezer paper

Water-soluble glue stick

Stapler

*If you want to use the same red print for the blocks and binding, you'll need ⅞ yard total.

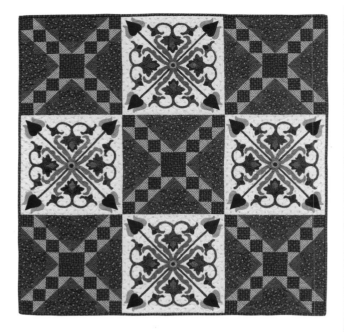

CUTTING

From the cream print, cut:
4 squares, 17" x 17"

From *each* of the yellow and green prints, cut:
5 strips, 2⅞" x 42"; crosscut into 60 squares,
    2⅞" x 2⅞"

From the red print for pieced blocks, cut:
5 strips, 2½" x 42"; crosscut into 80 squares,
    2½" x 2½"

From the blue print, cut:
3 strips, 2½" x 42"; crosscut into 40 squares,
    2½" x 2½"

3 strips, 4½" x 42"; crosscut into 40 rectangles,
    2½" x 4½"

From the green wool, cut:
16 stems, ¼" x 8"

From the red print for binding, cut:
6 strips, 2¼" x 42"

PREPARING FOR APPLIQUÉ

1. Fold each cream 17" square in half diagonally in both directions and finger-press the folds. Fold each square in half vertically and horizontally, and finger-press the folds. If desired, mark over the fold lines with a water-soluble pen.

2. Refer to "Making a Master Pattern" (page 6) to make a master pattern using the patterns on page 71.

3. Refer to "Making the Appliqués" (page 6) to trace all of the appliqué shapes onto freezer paper, roughly cut out the shapes, and then iron the freezer-paper shapes onto your chosen colors of wool. You will need four sets of appliqués for the blocks. Refer to the photo above left and the materials list for fabric choices as needed. Cut out the wool shapes.

ADDING THE APPLIQUÉS

1. Refer to "Appliquéing Wool to the Background" (page 7) to position the appliqué on each of the background squares. Working from the bottom layer to the top, glue and staple your prepared appliqué pieces in place.

2. Using your thread and needle of choice, appliqué the pieces in place with a blanket stitch (page 8). Remove the staples.

3. Trim the blocks to measure 16½" x 16½", keeping the design centered.

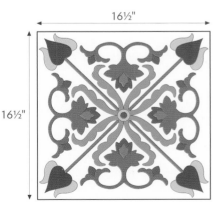

MAKING THE PIECED BLOCKS

1. Refer to "Half-Square-Triangle Units" (page 11). Using the 60 yellow and 60 green 2⅞" squares, make 120 half-square-triangle units. Press the seam allowances toward the darker triangles.

Make 120.

2. Arrange six half-square-triangle units, four red 2½" squares, two blue 2½" squares, and two blue 2½" x 4½" rectangles into four rows as shown. Sew the pieces into rows and press the seam allowances in opposite directions from row to row. Sew the rows together. Make 10 of these units. Repeat to make 10 mirror-image units. Wait until the next step to press the seam allowances, or press them open.

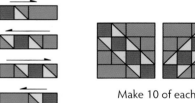
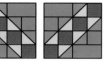

Make 10 of each.

3. Arrange four units together as shown to make a block. Press the seam allowances so they will be in opposite directions when the units are joined. Sew the units together and press the seam allowances as shown. Make five blocks.

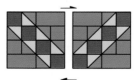
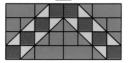
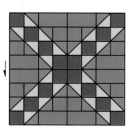

Make 5.

ASSEMBLING THE QUILT TOP

1. Arrange the blocks into three rows of three blocks each as shown. Sew the blocks into rows. Press the seam allowances toward the appliquéd blocks.

2. Sew the three rows together. Press the seam allowances toward the center row.

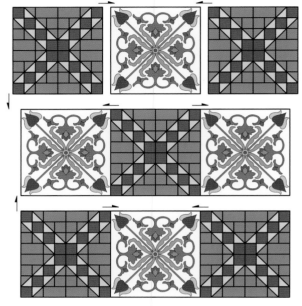

Quilt assembly

FINISHING

1. Cut and piece the backing fabric so it's 4" larger than the quilt top on each side. Sandwich the batting between the backing and quilt top, and baste the layers together.

2. Quilt as desired. Deirdre machine quilted an allover design.

3. Trim the backing and batting even with the quilt top. Refer to "Binding" (page 13) to bind the quilt edges with the red 2¼"-wide strips.

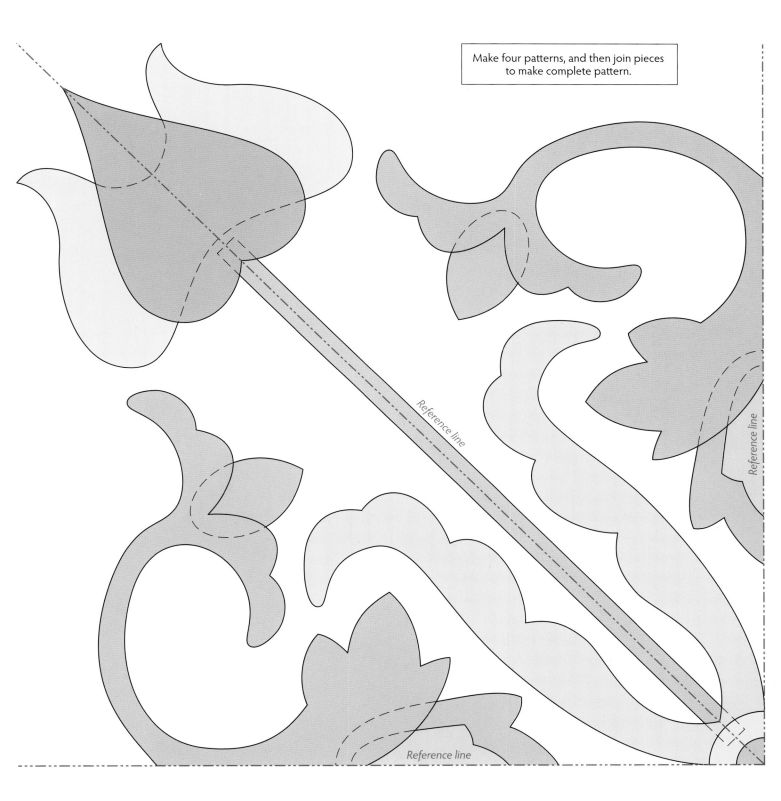

Make four patterns, and then join pieces
to make complete pattern.

Reference line

Reference line

Reference line

RHUBARB AND CUSTARD

When I saw these two beautiful prints, I immediately envisioned a design with a positive and negative image. I knew I wanted to use them in this simple way. For the flowers and leaves, I chose two colors of wool that complemented the prints. I love pieced basket blocks and thought it would be fun to make large ones forming the background for the appliqué. The colors of this quilt remind me of a favorite dessert that my Nanna made for us as children—rhubarb and custard.

~ Deirdre

FINISHED QUILT: 50" x 50"
FINISHED BLOCKS: 18" x 18"

"Rhubarb and Custard," designed, machine pieced, hand appliquéd, and machine quilted by Deirdre Bond-Abel

MATERIALS

Cotton Fabric

Yardage is based on 42"-wide fabric.

1¾ yards of terra-cotta print for sashing and binding

1⅓ yards *each* of red print and yellow print for blocks and sawtooth sashing

3⅓ yards of fabric for backing

Felted Wool Fabric

Yardage is based on 48"-wide fabric

⅓ yard *each* of rust and yellow for appliqués

Additional Materials

Embroidery floss in colors to match wool fabrics

58" x 58" piece of batting

36" length of freezer paper

Water-soluble glue stick

Stapler

CUTTING

From *each* of the red and yellow prints cut:

2 squares, 19" x 19"

2 squares, 8½" x 8½"

5 strips, 2½" x 42"; crosscut into 72 squares, 2½" x 2½"

Continued on page 74

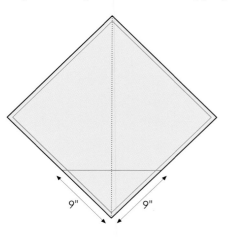

Continued from page 73

From the terra-cotta print, cut:

3 strips, 6½" x 42"; crosscut into:

    1 square, 6½" x 6½"

    4 rectangles, 4½" x 6½"

    36 rectangles, 2½" x 6½"

5 strips, 4½" x 42"; crosscut into:

    4 squares, 4½" x 4½"

    72 rectangles, 2½" x 4½"

6 strips, 2¼" x 42"

From *each* of the rust and yellow wool pieces, cut:

2 strips, ¼" x 12"

4 strips, ¼" x 6"

4 strips, ¼" x 1"

PREPARING FOR APPLIQUÉ

1. Fold each red and yellow 19" square in half diagonally once and finger-press the fold. If desired, mark over the fold lines with a water-soluble marker.

2. Lightly mark a line ½" from the edge of the 19" squares on all four sides, this will be your finished edge and will also be a reference line for the pattern.

3. Turn the block on point and measure 9" from the bottom corner on two sides. Lightly draw a line from one point to the other. This line will be covered by the top edge of the large triangle and will help with the placement of the appliqué.

4. Refer to "Making a Master Pattern" (page 6) to make a master pattern using the pattern pieces on pages 77–79.

5. Refer to "Making the Appliqués" (page 6) to trace all of the appliqué shapes onto freezer paper, roughly cut out the shapes, and then iron the freezer-paper shapes onto the felted wool. You will need two sets of red and two sets of yellow appliqué shapes.

ADDING THE APPLIQUÉS AND CORNER TRIANGLES

1. Position a background square over your master pattern and pin the two together making sure that the diagonal center line and the triangle placement line on the fabric is matching up with the corresponding lines on the pattern.

2. Refer to "Appliquéing Wool to the Background" (page 7) to position the appliqué on each of the background squares. In this design, none of the shapes overlap each other, so it doesn't matter where you start. Just make sure that the bottom ends of the stems extend below the triangle placement line.

3. Using your thread and needle of choice, appliqué the pieces in place with a blanket stitch (page 8). Remove the staples.

4. Trim the blocks to measure 18½" square, making sure that the design remains centered.

5. Draw a diagonal line from corner to corner on the wrong side of each of the red and yellow 8½" squares.

6. Referring to "Quick Corner Triangles" (page 11), position a marked square right sides together on an appliquéd block, lining up the outside edges and making sure that the drawn line on the smaller square is aligned with the drawn line on the larger square. Sew on the line and press the resulting triangle toward the corner, making sure the edges are aligned with the square underneath. Fold back the top triangle and trim the outside corner, leaving a ¼" seam allowance. Press the seam allowances toward the triangle. Repeat this process with the remaining blocks.

MAKING THE SASHING STRIPS

1. Draw a diagonal line from corner to corner on the wrong side of each of the red and yellow 2½" squares.

2. Referring to "Quick Corner Triangles" (page 11), sew a marked red square to the right side of a terra-cotta 2½" x 6½" rectangle and a marked yellow square to the left side of the rectangle. Make sure the angles are the same as shown in the diagram. Make 18.

Make 18.

3. Repeat step 2, but place the squares on opposite ends of the rectangles. Make 18.

Make 18.

4. Sew nine of the units together as shown to make a sashing row. Press the seam allowances in one direction. Make two with the units from step 2 and two with the units from step 3.

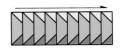

Make 2 of each.

5. Sew a marked yellow 2½" square to a terra-cotta 2½" x 4½" rectangle as shown. Press the seam allowances toward the triangle. Make 18. Repeat to sew red squares to terra-cotta 2½" x 4½" rectangles to make 18. Make 18 of each with the squares on the opposite side of the rectangles.

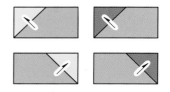

Make 18 of each.

6. Join nine of the units from step 5 as shown to make sashing strips for the outer edges of the quilt.

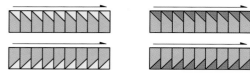

Make 2 of each.

ASSEMBLING THE QUILT TOP

1. Arrange the four appliquéd blocks with two center sashing strips as shown. Make sure that the small red triangles are adjacent to large red triangles and the small yellow triangles are next to the large yellow triangles. Sew the blocks and sashing strips together and press the seam allowances toward the appliquéd blocks.

2. Sew the two remaining center sashing strips to the terra-cotta 6½" square as shown. Press the seam allowances toward the square.

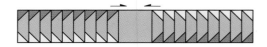

3. Sew the sashing strip from step 2 between the two rows of blocks to make the quilt center. Press the seam allowances toward the appliquéd blocks.

4. Sew the terra-cotta 4½" x 6½" rectangles between the outer sashing units as shown. Add a terra-cotta 4½" square to each end of two sashing strips. Press the seam allowances toward the terra-cotta rectangles and squares.

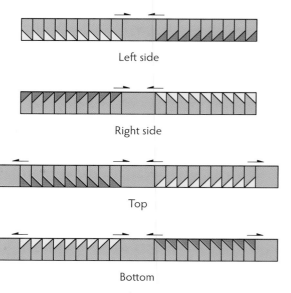

Left side

Right side

Top

Bottom

5. Sew the two sashing strips without end squares to the sides of the quilt center. Press the seam allowances toward the quilt center. Sew the two remaining sashing strips to the top and bottom of the quilt center and press the seam allowances toward the quilt center.

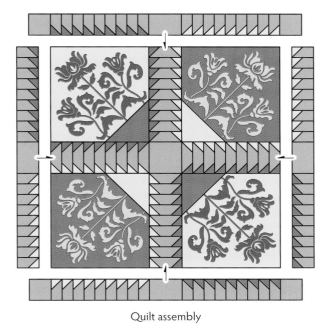

Quilt assembly

FINISHING

1. Cut and piece the backing fabric so it's 4" larger than the quilt top on each side. Sandwich the batting between the backing and the quilt top, and baste the layers together.

2. Quilt as desired. Deirdre machine quilted an allover swirling design.

3. Trim the backing and batting even with the quilt edge. Refer to "Binding" (page 13) to bind the quilt with the terra-cotta 2¼"-wide strips.

Align with pattern on page 79.

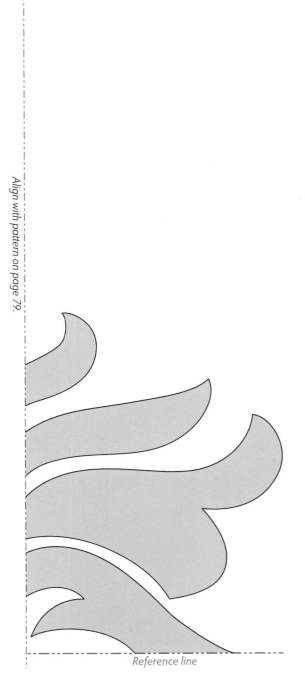

Reference line

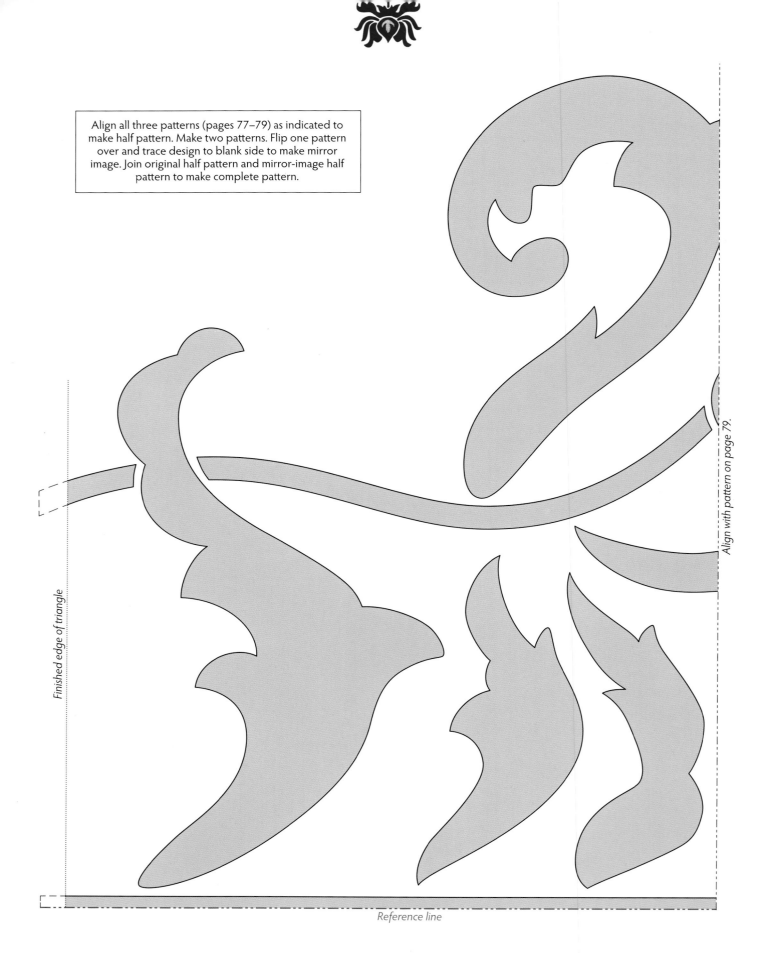

Align all three patterns (pages 77–79) as indicated to make half pattern. Make two patterns. Flip one pattern over and trace design to blank side to make mirror image. Join original half pattern and mirror-image half pattern to make complete pattern.

Finished edge of triangle

Align with pattern on page 79.

Reference line

Align with pattern on page 78.

Align with pattern on page 77.

Reference line

Rhubarb and Custard

BELLINGHAM

Medallion settings are probably my favorites to design. For this quilt, I used one of my favorite blocks as well—the Churn Dash—to fill in between the appliqués. I wanted the quilt to look rich, scrappy, and antique. I was working on this quilt when Leonie and I had a wonderful holiday with friends in the state of Washington. They took us for a drive to a town called Bellingham and I fell in love with it. I named this quilt after that beautiful place.

~ Deirdre

FINISHED QUILT: 72" x 88"
FINISHED BLOCKS: 8" x 8"

"Bellingham," designed, machine pieced, hand appliquéd, and machine quilted by Deirdre Bond-Abel

MATERIALS

Cotton Fabric

Yardage is based on 42"-wide fabric.

2⅜ yards of cream print for appliqué background*

1⅞ yards of dark-blue print for setting blocks

4" x 42" strip *each* of 34 assorted prints for pieced blocks

⅔ yard of green print for binding

5½ yards of fabric for backing

*If your fabric is less than 41" wide after removing selvages, you'll need 2⅔ yards.

Felted Wool Fabric

Center Block

4" x 4" piece of teal for flower 1A

4" x 7" piece of cherry red for flower 1B

5" x 6" piece of dull red for flower 1C

5" x 6" piece of dark teal for flower 1D

8" x 12" piece of textured red for flower 2A

6" x 6" piece of dark blue for flower 2B

6" x 10" piece of light blue for flower 3A

7" x 7" piece of medium for flower 3B

5" x 5" piece of dark blue for flower 3C

3" x 3" piece of dark red for flower 3D

12" x 16" piece of brown for stem base A

6" x 6" piece of tan herringbone for stem base B

3" x 4" piece of dark teal for stem base C

8" x 18" piece of olive green for leaf 1

8" x 40" piece of green for leaf 2

16" x 16" piece of tan for side stem base

4" x 12" piece of brown for stems

Continued on page 82

CUTTING

From the cream print, cut:
1 rectangle, 25" x 41"
2 strips, 25" x 42"; crosscut into 8 rectangles, 9" x 25"

From the dark-blue print, cut:
7 strips, 8½" x 42"; crosscut into 26 squares, 8½" x 8½"

From *each* of the 34 assorted prints, cut:
4 squares, 3⅞" x 3⅞"
5 squares, 2½" x 2½"
4 rectangles, 1½" x 2½"

From the green print, cut:
9 strips, 2¼" x 42"

From the brown wool for center block, cut:
4 stems, ¼" x 12"
6 stems, ¼" x 7"

From the green wool for borders, cut:
16 stems, ¼" x 7"
16 stems, ¼" x 6"

PREPARING FOR APPLIQUÉ

1. For the center block, fold the cream 25" x 41" rectangle in half vertically and horizontally and finger-press the folds. If desired, mark over the fold lines with a water-soluble marker.

2. For each of the eight border strips, fold the cream 9" x 25" rectangles in half vertically and finger-press the folds. Mark in the same manner as the center block. Lightly draw a line ⅝" from the edge down one long side of each strip; this will be used for positioning the fabric.

3. Refer to "Making a Master Pattern" (page 6) to make a master pattern using the patterns on pages 85–90. You will need to trace the two halves of the design for the center block and two halves of the design for the border appliqué.

Continued from page 81

Borders

¼ yard of brown for stem base A
4" x 8" piece of tan herringbone for stem base B
3" x 6" piece of dark teal for stem base C
10" x 20" piece of rust for flower 1A
8" x 8" piece of bright teal for flower 1B
12" x 12" piece of light blue for flower 2A
10" x 10" piece of medium blue for flower 2B
8" x 8" piece of dark blue for flower 2C
6" x 6" piece of dark red for flower 2D
8" x 8" piece of tan for leaf 1
8" x 16" piece of green for leaf 2
8" x 10" piece of green for stems

Additional Materials

Embroidery floss in colors to match wool fabrics
80" x 96" piece of batting
72" length of freezer paper
Water-soluble glue stick
Stapler

4. Refer to "Making the Appliqués" (page 6) to trace all of the appliqué shapes onto freezer paper, roughly cut out the shapes, and then iron the freezer-paper shapes onto your chosen colors of wool. Cut out two sets of shapes for the center block and eight sets for the border appliqué. Refer to the photo on page 80 and the materials list for fabric choices as needed. Cut out the wool shapes.

ADDING THE APPLIQUÉS

1. Refer to "Appliquéing Wool to the Background" (page 7). Position the curving stems first, and then add the flower segments, working from the bottom layer to the top. Add the base of the stems, and then the leaves.

2. Unpin the fabric from the master pattern and turn the fabric around, repositioning it over the master pattern, and then add the other half of the appliqué.

3. For the border appliqué, position the background fabric over the master pattern, lining up the center and side line with the reference lines on the master pattern.

4. Position the border appliqués, and then staple in place.

5. Using your thread and needle of choice, appliqué the pieces in place with a blanket stitch (page 8). Remove the staples.

6. Trim the center block to measure 24½" x 40½" and the border sections to measure 8½" x 24½".

MAKING THE PIECED BLOCKS

There are 34 pieced blocks with two fabrics in each block. Group the 34 fabrics into 17 pairs to make two blocks from each pair, reversing the position of the fabrics in the second block. The steps are written to make two blocks at a time.

1. Choose a pair of fabrics, and referring to "Half-Square-Triangle Units" (page 11), place the four 3⅞" squares from each fabric right sides together to make eight half-square-triangle units. Press the seam allowances toward the darker triangle.

Make 8.

2. Sew a 1½" x 2½" rectangle to the sides of four 2½" squares and press the seam allowances toward the darker print. Make four of each combination.

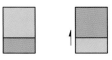

Make 4 of each.

3. Arrange and sew the units into rows. Press the seam allowances toward the units from step 2.

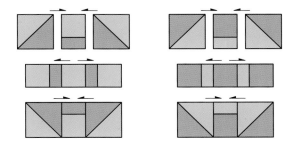

4. Sew the three rows together to finish the blocks and press the seam allowances toward the center row.

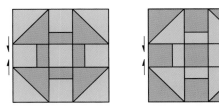

5. Repeat the steps with each pair of fabrics to make a total of 34 blocks.

ASSEMBLING THE QUILT TOP

1. Sew a dark-blue setting block to the right side of a pieced block to make a short row and press the seam allowances toward the setting block. Make 24.

2. Sew five units together in a checkerboard pattern, pressing the seam allowances in one direction. Make two of these side border units.

3. Sew the border units from step 2 to the sides of the center appliquéd block and press the seam allowances toward the center block.

4. Sew seven units from step 1 together to make a top border unit. Make a second unit for the bottom.

5. Sew the top and bottom border units to the quilt center. Press the seam allowances toward the quilt center.

6. Make the side borders by sewing two pieced blocks, a setting block, and two appliquéd border rectangles together as shown. Press the seam allowances toward the setting square and appliquéd rectangles. Make two and sew to the sides of the quilt. Press the seam allowances toward the border.

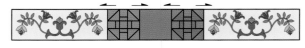

Side borders

7. Make the top and bottom borders by sewing three pieced blocks and two appliquéd border rectangles together as shown. Press the seam allowances toward the appliquéd rectangles. Make two and sew these to the top and bottom of the quilt. Press the seam allowances toward the border.

Quilt assembly

FINISHING

1. Cut and piece the backing fabric so it's 4" larger than the quilt top on each side. Sandwich the batting between the backing and the quilt top, and baste the layers together.

2. Quilt as desired. Deirdre machine quilted an allover design.

3. Trim the backing and batting even with the quilt edge. Refer to "Binding" (page 13) to bind the quilt edges with the green 2¼"-wide strips.

Border Pattern

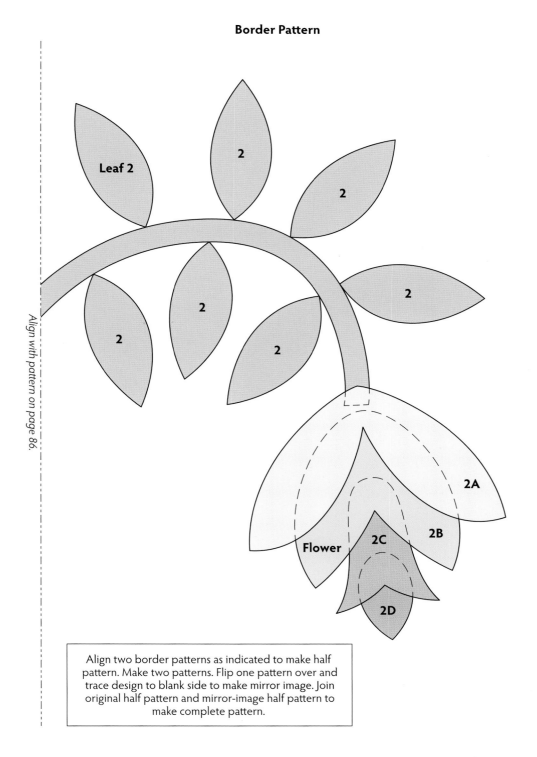

Align with pattern on page 86.

Align two border patterns as indicated to make half pattern. Make two patterns. Flip one pattern over and trace design to blank side to make mirror image. Join original half pattern and mirror-image half pattern to make complete pattern.

Border Pattern

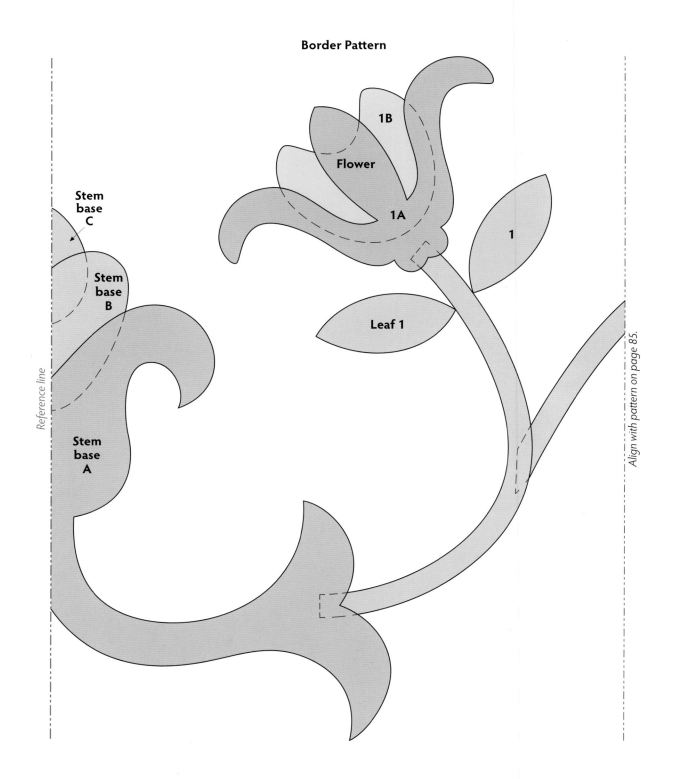

Center Pattern

Align all four center patterns as indicated to make half pattern. Make two patterns. Flip one pattern over and trace design to blank side to make mirror image. Join original half pattern and mirror-image half pattern to make complete pattern.

Flower

1B

1A

1C

1D

Reference line

Align with pattern on page 88.

Leaf 1

Appliqué assembly diagram

Center stems

1

1

1

Align with pattern on page 89.

Center Pattern

Align with pattern on page 87.

2B

Flower

2A

Leaf 2

2

2

2

2

2

Side
stem

2

2

2

Align with pattern on page 90.

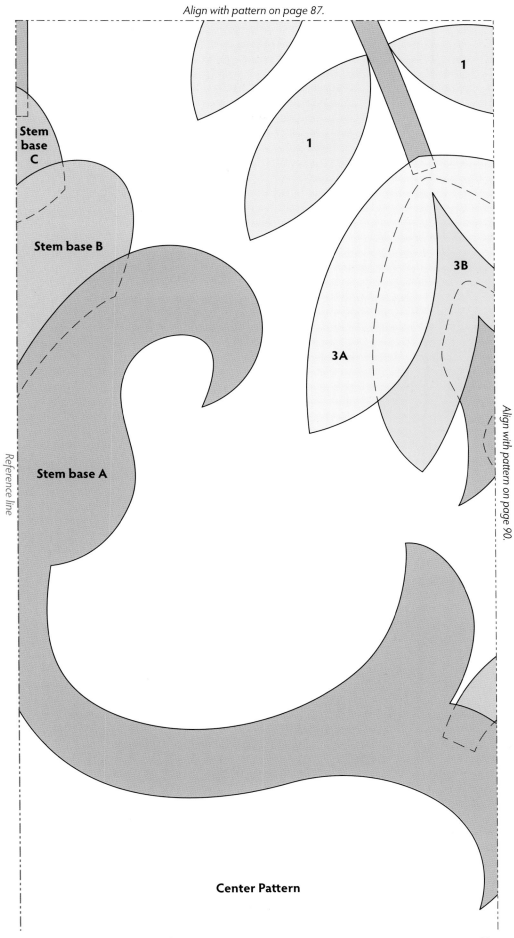

Stem
base
C

Stem base B

1

1

1

3B

3A

Align with pattern on page 90.

Reference line

Stem base A

Center Pattern

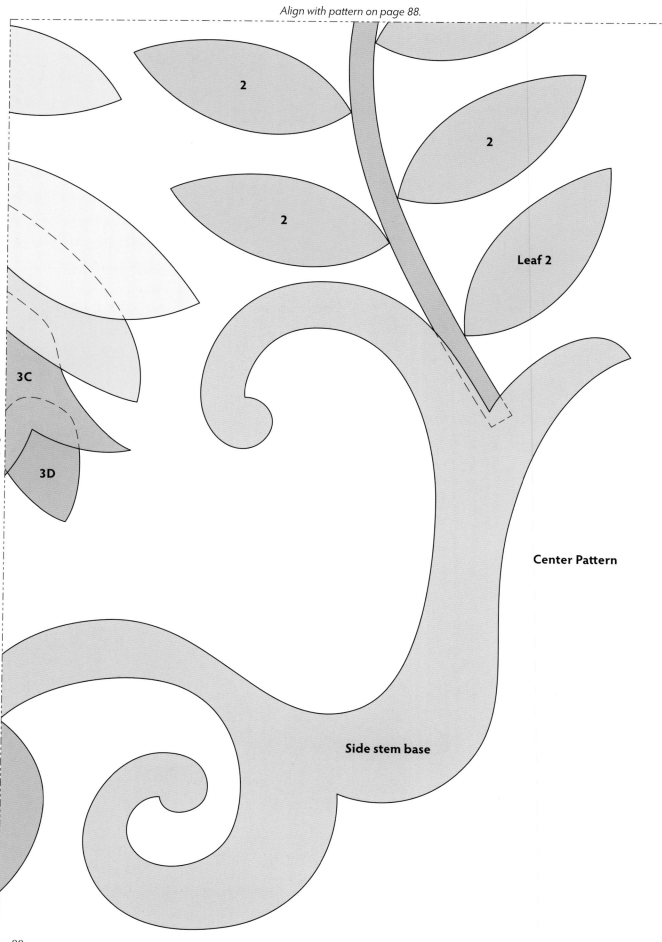

Align with pattern on page 89.

2

2

2

Leaf 2

3C

3D

Center Pattern

Side stem base

OUT ON THE TILES

The designs on ceramic tiles are a wonderful source of inspiration. I've incorporated a tile-like shape for the appliqué on this simple table runner and added a beautiful paisley print into the cutout area to give extra color and pattern. This simple and quick project would make an ideal gift for a friend or family member.

~ Deirdre

FINISHED RUNNER: 16" x 40"

"Out on the Tiles," designed, machine pieced, hand appliquéd, and machine quilted by Deirdre Bond-Abel

MATERIALS

Cotton Fabric

Yardage is based on 42"-wide fabric.

⅝ yard of red print for border and binding

½ yard of cream print for appliquéd-block background and border

1 fat quarter of paisley print for reverse-appliqué inserts

1½ yards of fabric for backing

Felted Wool Fabric

10" x 38" piece of burgundy for appliqués

Additional Materials

Embroidery floss in colors to match wool fabric

24" x 48" piece of batting

20" length of freezer paper

Water-soluble glue stick

Stapler

CUTTING

From the cream print, cut:
1 rectangle, 13" x 37"
4 rectangles, 2½" x 4½"

From the red print, cut:
4 strips, 2½" x 42"; crosscut into:
    4 strips, 2½" x 18½"
    4 rectangles, 2½" x 4½"
    12 squares, 2½" x 2½"
3 strips, 2¼" x 42"

From the paisley print, cut:
1 rectangle, 8" x 10"
2 rectangles, 7" x 8"

PREPARING FOR APPLIQUÉ

1. Fold the cream 13" x 37" rectangle in half vertically and horizontally and finger-press the folds. If desired, mark over the fold lines with a water-soluble marker.

2. Refer to "Making a Master Pattern" (page 6) to make a master pattern using the patterns on pages 94 and 95.

3. Refer to "Making the Appliqués" (page 6) to trace the three appliqué shapes onto freezer paper, roughly cut out the shapes, and then iron the freezer-paper shapes onto the felted wool.

4. Refer to "Reverse Appliqué" (page 9) to appliqué the cutout sections in the burgundy wool.

5. Glue and staple the cotton rectangles right side down to the backs of the wool shapes.

6. Using embroidery thread and a blanket stitch (page 8), stitch around the edges of the cutout shapes. Remove the staples and trim the cotton fabric so that you can't see any of it from the front of the wool.

ADDING THE APPLIQUÉS

1. Refer to "Appliquéing Wool to the Background" (page 7) to position the appliqués on the background. Position the larger shape in the middle, lining up the two side points of the appliqué with the horizontal line on the background fabric and the center indented curve with the vertical line on the fabric. Position a smaller shape on each side, again using the horizontal line for reference and leaving a ¼" space between the side points. Glue and staple your prepared appliqué pieces in place.

2. Using embroidery thread and a blanket stitch, stitch around the outside edges of the appliqué shapes. Remove the staples.

3. Trim the background fabric to measure 12½" x 36½".

ASSEMBLING THE TABLE RUNNER

1. Draw a diagonal line from corner to corner on the wrong side of the red 2½" squares. Referring to "Quick Corner Triangles" (page 11), place marked red squares on opposite ends of a cream 2½" x 4½" rectangle. Sew on the marked lines. Trim the seam allowances to ¼". Press the triangles toward the corners. Make four flying-geese units.

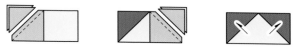

Make 4.

2. Use this same method to sew the remaining four red 2½" squares to each corner of the appliqué background.

3. Sew a red 2½" x 4½" rectangle to each side of a flying-geese unit and press the seam allowances toward the red rectangles. Make two.

Make 2.

4. Sew these two strips to the short sides of the runner and press the seam allowances toward the border.

5. Sew a red 2½" x 18½" strip to each side of the remaining two flying-geese units and press the seam allowances toward the red strips.

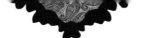

6. Sew these two strips to the long sides of the runner and press the seam allowances toward the border.

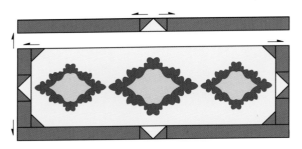

FINISHING

1. Cut the backing fabric so it's 4" larger than the table-runner top on each side. Sandwich the batting between the backing and the runner, and baste the layers together.

2. Quilt as desired. Deirdre machine quilted an allover meandering design.

3. Trim the backing and batting even with the runner top. Refer to "Binding" (page 13) to bind the runner edges using the red 2¼"-wide strips.

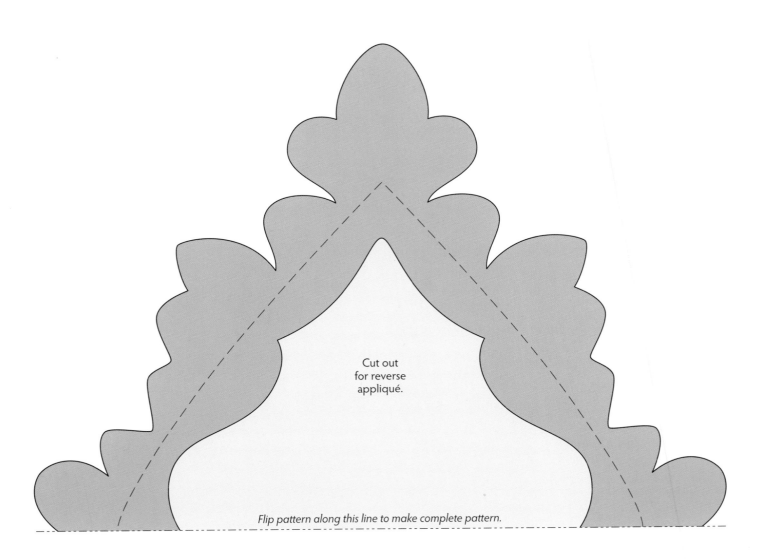

Cut out
for reverse
appliqué.

Flip pattern along this line to make complete pattern.

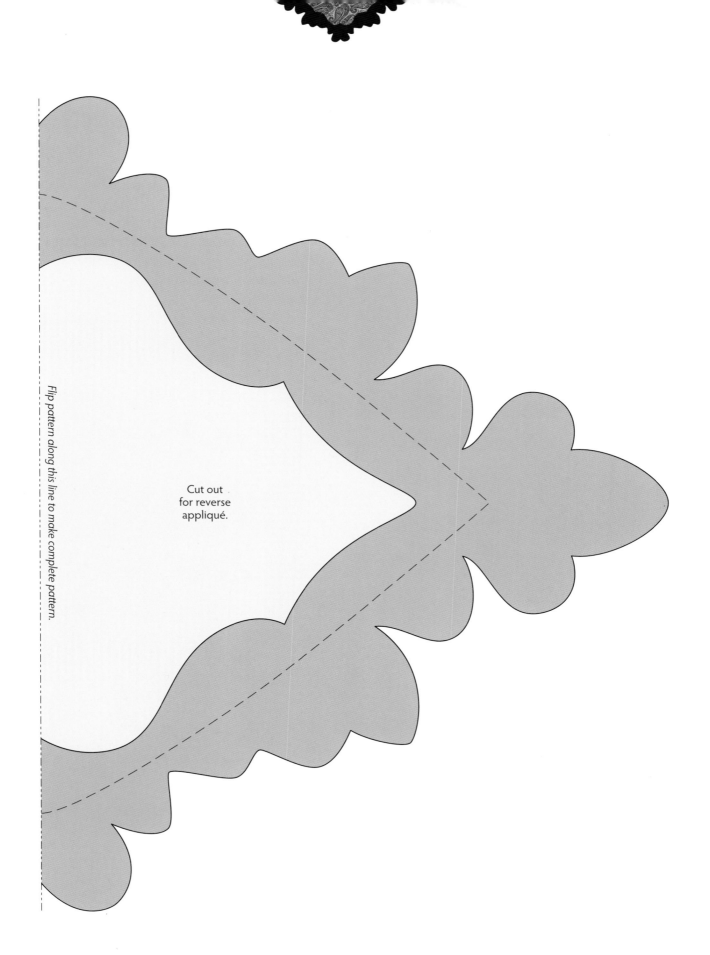

Flip pattern along this line to make complete pattern.

Cut out
for reverse
appliqué.

Leonie (left) and Deirdre (right)

Leonie has had a love of sewing for as long as she can remember. Her first attempt at quilting was just after her eldest daughter was born, and from then on she has never looked back. Most of what she does she has taught herself along the way through trial and error, reading books, and attending classes here and there. One of her dreams was to one day have her own quilt shop—a dream that she realized in 2005. She shares the quilt shop, The Quilted Crow, with her best friend, Deirdre, "the other crow." Leonie is married to Dan and has two beautiful daughters, Ellen and Jess. She lives in Hobart, Tasmania, Australia.

Deirdre is married and the mother to two beautiful children. In her former life she was a nurse who dreamed of being a quilt-shop owner. For many years now, she has been designing her own quilts to keep and to teach quilting. She joined forces in 2005 with her best friend, Leonie, to become one half of The Quilted Crow. Her family, animals, quilting, antiques, and music are her passions. What she loves most is sharing her love of wool appliqué with other like-minded people. Visit The Quilted Crow at www.TheQuiltedCrow.com.au.